The Book Industry

A REPORT OF THE PUBLIC LIBRARY INQUIRY OF

THE SOCIAL SCIENCE RESEARCH COUNCIL

A REPORT OF THE PUBLIC LIBRARY INQUIRY

The Book Industry

By William Miller

1949

COLUMBIA UNIVERSITY PRESS • NEW YORK

THIS PUBLICATION WAS MADE POSSIBLE BY FUNDS GRANTED BY CARNEGIE CORPORA-
TION OF NEW YORK TO THE SOCIAL SCIENCE RESEARCH COUNCIL FOR THE PUBLIC
LIBRARY INQUIRY. THE CARNEGIE CORPORATION IS NOT, HOWEVER, THE AUTHOR,
OWNER, PUBLISHER, OR PROPRIETOR OF THIS PUBLICATION, AND IS NOT TO BE UNDER-
STOOD AS APPROVING BY VIRTUE OF ITS GRANT ANY OF THE STATEMENTS MADE OR
VIEWS EXPRESSED THEREIN.

THE PUBLIC LIBRARY
INQUIRY

THE AMERICAN LIBRARY ASSOCIATION proposed to the Social Science Research Council, in 1946, that the Council "conduct a thorough and comprehensive study of the American free public library." The proposal further defined the nature of the study as "an appraisal in sociological, cultural and human terms . . . of the extent to which the libraries are achieving their objectives" and of the library's "potential and actual contribution to American society."

The Council approved the project and submitted to the Carnegie Corporation a proposal for a two-and-a-quarter-year study, to terminate in a general, final report in June, 1949. The inquiry was designed to use, insofar as possible in the study of the public library, such techniques and experience as social scientists have accumulated for the analysis of other social institutions. The Carnegie Corporation appropriated a total of $200,000 for support of the study.

The Council selected a director to be responsible for the conduct of the Inquiry and for the preparation of a final, general report, and to serve as editor of such reports on special aspects of the study as he recommends for separate publication.

A committee was appointed for the Inquiry to serve in an advisory, deliberative, and consultative capacity, under the chairmanship of the director. The Committee has reviewed and criticized the general report and the other Inquiry reports recommended for publication. The interpretations, judgments, and conclusions contained in them, however, are made solely on the authors' responsibility.

LILLIAN ORDEN, formerly with the U.S. Bureau of the Budget.

Foreign and International Developments: RICHARD H. HEINDEL, U.S. Senate Committee on Foreign Relations.

Mass Media: JOSEPH T. KLAPPER, Bureau of Applied Social Research.

Music Materials: OTTO LUENING, Professor of Music, Columbia University; assisted by H. R. Shawhan, and Eloise Moore.

Government Publications: JAMES L. MC CAMY, Professor of Political Science, University of Wisconsin; assisted by Julia B. McCamy.

Book Publishing: WILLIAM MILLER, writer and historian.

Library Processes: WATSON O'D. PIERCE, formerly Vice President, Nejelski & Company

Special Projects: HELEN R. ROBERTS, formerly with the Commission on Freedom of the Press.

Films: GLORIA WALDRON, Twentieth Century Fund; assisted by Cecile Starr.

Administrative Assistant: LOIS A. MURKLAND.

FOREWORD

AMERICAN PUBLIC LIBRARIES, in seeking to meet the varied needs of a democratic people, have for some time been collecting and lending music, films, paintings, and other creative work and informative materials. Yet their main stock in trade remains the printed book. Librarians, therefore, have a vital interest in the book industry; any factor which influences the nature and availability of books must, in the long run, deeply affect the services rendered by libraries to the public.

The major book sources in this country are the university presses, the publishing agencies of the government, and the commercial book publishers. Simultaneously with the Public Library Inquiry, Chester Kerr, for the Association of American University Presses, conducted a survey of the business and editorial activities of the university publishers. A study of the production, distribution, and editing of government documents has been made by James L. McCamy for the Public Library Inquiry. William Miller, in this study, writes of commercial book publishing.

With critical acumen, Mr. Miller analyzes the present conditions and trends in the trade-book industry. In some respects his book brings Cheney's *Survey* of 1930–31 up to date, though that has not been his special aim. Mr. Miller's study concerns the book industry today and what may be expected of it tomorrow. He does not attempt to describe the structure or day-to-day operations of the industry, except in so far as important changes are affecting them, and he places strongest emphasis upon the consequences for editorial policy of modern publishing conditions. In so doing he has the advantages gained from his own experience in the field and from an earlier study of the industry which he wrote for *Fortune*, November, 1943.

Mr. Miller makes it plain that the relations between public libraries and the publishing industry are in a sense one-sided. This results from the simple fact that public libraries purchase only a small proportion of the ordinary sales output of publishers. Hence, while the book industry is vital to libraries, the latter are less essential to the industry.

Under these circumstances, public libraries can hardly exert any large influence over book production and distribution. But they can exert some influence, an appreciable amount at certain points, and they may, by making changes in their own approaches to the publishing problem, be able to extend their influence further. In order to do so, libraries must formulate their own aims and then gain some insight into the degree in which book-industry trends are favorable and the degree in which they are inimical to those aims. The present study is well calculated to supply such insight.

From extended personal observation and study, and with the consensus of trade publisher judgment behind him, Mr. Miller finds the outlook gloomy for the serious literature that is the lifeblood of the library. Mr. Miller's analysis of the growing importance of the mass market, with its concentration upon best sellers and its close affiliation with book clubs, cheap reprints, the movies, and other heretofore "subsidiary" agencies—a concentration made stronger by the pressure of rising costs, especially for the small edition—is a statement no person interested in the country's literary and civic health can read complacently. The problem is of direct importance to librarians.

The solution for the libraries is not to be found in any simple publisher-library agreement. As Mr. Miller recognizes, all changes in the relation of public libraries to the book industry must take place in an area whose ultimate limits are beyond the immediate control of either publisher or librarian; that is, within the framework set by the literacy and social circumstances obtaining among the American people as a whole. Yet, small as the book industry itself is, and even smaller though the library influence is, the stakes are high, and what improvement is possible should be attempted.

The study, based on first-hand observation and direct testimony, provides a picture of one aspect of the public library's interests which is peculiarly pertinent to its more serious objectives. More than this, it should be enlightening to all those outside the library world who are concerned with the book industry as a factor in mass-communication in American society.

ROBERT D. LEIGH

New York
June, 1949

CONTENTS

The Book Industry

I

TRADE PUBLISHING
A GENERAL VIEW

IT IS NOT TRUE that the American book publishing industry is chronically sicker than other industries, but it is often written about as if it were. In this, as in other respects, it resembles that other die-hard, the Broadway theater. Neither book business nor show business is ever so healthy that it is uninteresting, but both have outlived generations of mourners.

Book industry Cassandras have not lacked for themes; if the pirating of foreign titles was not going to kill the industry, price cutting was; if not price cutting, then free libraries; if not libraries, book clubs; if not clubs, 25-cent books. A recent menace has been high manufacturing costs. To hear some book people tell it, each new bogey must have been more terrible than the last. Yet many of the developments that from time to time were going to kill the industry actually made it grow. Book business today, though below its peak of 1946, remains much bigger in copy and dollar volume than in any prewar year—bigger and at least in that sense better for publishers, manufacturers, distributors, and authors.

Yet there are problems facing American book publishing and threats to its continued health and expansion. Trade book publishing, with which the public libraries and hence this segment of the Public Library Inquiry are most concerned, probably faces more difficult problems than does any other branch. The most difficult of these lie outside the industry and cannot be solved by it alone. They stem from certain key circumstances in American history, such as Negro slavery, the sparse settlement of the early West, the growth and concentration of corporate and church power, the movement of higher-income urban dwellers to suburbs free of city taxes. These and related conditions continue to shape American life today. Their impact upon the book industry is felt most directly in the form of inadequate government expenditures for the education, in schools and libraries, of sizable portions of the population and in the form of business, religious, and political pressures that result in the censorship and intimidation of writers, editors, and publishers.

About these conditions and their causes the American book publishing industry can do little but issue books that disclose them. There remains the problem of getting such books bought and read. American book publishers know that book buying is a function of book reading, that reading is a function of education, and that education, at least on the higher levels, is a function of income. But the publishers cannot raise the standard of living of the poor and unenlightened who are now cut off from the book market, nor can the publishers alone raise the general level of education so that more people who now buy some books may become more active buyers and readers of serious works. Some years ago a committee of book publishers agreed that "salability as well as merit must inevitably influence a publisher's decisions" in making his list; this decision implies a harsher criticism of American education and taste than of the publishers of American books.[1]

In many countries less enlightened and less cultured than

[1]Besides the problem of taste, there is the equally serious question of the availability of and interest in information to be used by citizens responsible for participating in public decisions. On the extent of public information on selected subjects see "Civic Enlightenment in the United States As Measured by Public Opinion Polling Agencies," by Helen R. Roberts (a mimeographed report to the Public Library Inquiry, July, 1948).

the United States the book market is thinner and poorer; in others, more modest than America in claims to education and culture, the reverse is true. American publishers and booksellers sometimes speak with wonder and envy of Denmark, Finland, Iceland, New Zealand, or Czechoslovakia, where prewar per capita book buying is said to have been much larger than it is here. Occasional reports on book publishing in these countries do not satisfactorily explain their superiority. Lack of free libraries and inexpensive magazines may be a factor; studies of prewar social and economic structures in these countries probably would disclose other reasons. As for America, I take it as a reflection on the general level of culture more than on the book industry that Adolph Kroch, who runs a distinguished book store (with three branches) in Chicago and a book section in a department store in Detroit, recently invested his savings in real estate because he could not find locations where new book stores attempting to sell the whole range of trade books might prosper.

Kroch may be atypical; actually, two or three hundred (nobody really knows how many) booksellers started in business in the United States between 1946 and 1948. But most of their enterprises were small, and if they follow American precedents those not in department stores or chains will soon be stamped "credit poor, collections slow" and will never improve that rating. Most remarkable, indeed, about bookseller Kroch is the fact that he had capital to invest; his failure to find opportunities for it in the book industry points up the social problems that face American book publishers and are the major threats to their welfare.

The social problems resulting in poor book towns and a poor book country are too complex to be dealt with further here; they are also too serious to be neglected. Only if they are dealt with promptly and earnestly by publishers and booksellers as well as they are able and by other social agencies can the American book publishing industry greatly improve its performance in a key role in a democratic state.

THE MEANING OF TRADE BOOKS   Though this study will touch upon other phases of the book industry, its main interest, as has been said, is in "trade books"—the industry's jargon for general literature, carried over from the time when such literature was issued almost exclusively by regular trade publishers and sold at their prices in regular book stores.

Originally the terms "trade books" and "trade titles" were roughly interchangeable, the latter simply referring to the names by which the former were called. Today, however, large printings of some trade titles are issued by companies not ordinarily considered trade publishers and are distributed at a wide range of cut-rate prices outside "regular trade" channels. The book clubs, for example, sell their editions direct to the reader and entirely by mail; other cheap reprints, produced by specialized reprint houses (which also issue some original books of their own), are sold over the counter in many types of retail establishments. Sometimes book club editions and other reprints of "trade titles" are included in the term "trade books"; at other times they are not. In this book, except where the context clearly indicates another meaning, "trade books" stands for trade titles in any or all editions. Figures given in Appendix B show that title-, copy-, or dollar-wise, trade books thus defined form the biggest part of American book production.

There remain other and older problems in identifying trade books which, as O. H. Cheney pointed out in a perspicacious survey of the book industry in 1930–31, attest to the haphazard ways in which trade publishers make up and try to sell their lists.

Too often the fact is overlooked [writes Cheney] that a trade-book list is a miscellaneous list with miscellaneous—and sometimes immiscible—problems. . . . Two publishers may, and often do, handle exactly the same type of book in two absolutely different ways. One may consider it a trade-book and sell it through retail channels and another may consider it a mail-order book to be offered to a special list of individuals. . . . Practically every one of the types of books on the general list of a publisher may be the type of product of a specialized publisher.[2]

Cheney, reporting to a predecessor of the American Book Publishers Council, made up largely of trade houses, solved his problem by saying simply that he had studied "the types of books published by the members." He also considered "specialized books such as technical, professional and religious," so for him these were *not* "trade books."[3] Ordinarily, neither are textbooks, scholarly and scientific monographs, manuals, annuals, or the publications of governments.

Though a few trade publishers give it little attention, fiction rules the trade-book world. Also included among trade books by virtually all trade publishers are history, biography, poetry, popular science and psychology, stories of family life, travel, and war, and personal books on public or private affairs. Sex is a staple trade-book subject and sells well in almost any literary form, as some very conservative trade houses rediscover from time to time, especially when they need cash. Even as technical a work as the Kinsey-Pomeroy-Martin *Sexual Behavior in the Human Male* was sought by many trade houses, and though issued by an austere medical house it became a best seller in trade-book stores. Some trade publishers then used it to suggest the contents of other books. Ziff Davis Publishing Company claimed, in advertising Emily Harvin's *The Stubborn Wood* in the New York *Herald Tribune*, March 10, 1948, that in this novel "Many of the facts

[2]O. H. Cheney, *Economic Survey of the Book Industry, 1930–1931; Final Report*, New York, National Association of Book Publishers, 1931, pp. 159–60.
[3]*Ibid.*, p. 2.

revealed in a book like the KINSEY REPORT are brought into sharp focus in the tortured life of a lovely, sensitive woman." Crown Publishers said in the same paper, April 4, 1948, that Hiram Haydn's novel *The Time Is Noon* was enthusiastically received, "not because it is about the ideas and the morals of young Americans just out of college in the 1920's . . . not even because it startles us, as did the Kinsey Report with an undraped portrayal of what we are really like. . . ."

Books for children and adolescents and staples such as cookbooks, gardening books, anthologies, and self-help books, and books of puzzles, games, and quizzes also are normally in the trade category. Steady income from such merchandise helps many publishers finance those fliers on adult fiction that give trade publishing its authentic tone, fiction with a best-seller and book club look and the promise of reprint, serial, movie, or digest sale.

In 1886, in an essay called "Why We Have No Great Novelists," H. H. Boyesen wrote that the woman reader is "the Iron Madonna who strangles in her fond embrace the American novelist."[4] The influence of women on trade books is still great. Few publishers or editors are women (except in the juvenile field), but on trade books more than on any other kind lies the stamp of the female literary agent, manuscript reader, book-shop manager, department store buyer, librarian, lecturer—and reader: a formidable gamut even for the writings of the most "queenly novelist," for which appellation many still compete.

Only trade books are likely to be promoted at book fairs, autographing parties, literary teas, and cocktail parties. A fortunate few are the subjects of Sunday and syndicated book section gossip, of reviews in the New York *Times* and *Herald*

[4] Arthur Meier Schlesinger, *The Rise of the City, 1878–1898*, New York, Macmillan, 1933, p. 249.

Tribune, Time, the *Atlantic, Harper's,* the *New Yorker,* and the *Saturday Review of Literature* and of the advertisements that make profitable the pages that carry such reviews.

THE DIVERSIFIED FIRMS   Yet to distinguish trade books from other publications is not necessarily to distinguish trade-book houses from the rest of the book publishing industry. This has been especially true in recent years, when a number of essentially nontrade houses, such as John Wiley & Sons and the D. Van Nostrand Co., shared in the trade-book boom and many trade publishers issued textbooks and technical books for wartime and postwar markets.

But even in normal times notable trade publishing is done by houses strong in other fields. Harper & Brothers, with text-books and business books, a medical affiliate, and a prosperous Bible and religious department, has a big and diversified trade list each year. So have Harcourt, Brace & Co. and the Houghton Mifflin Co., each an important publisher of college text-books. One of the most prominent trade houses is Chas. Scribner's Sons, publishers also of religious books and text-books. The J. B. Lippincott Co., with medical and technical lists, and Longmans, Green & Co., which issues religious books, are also notable trade houses. Old textbook firms, such as Henry Holt & Co. and Appleton-Century-Crofts, maintain trade departments that sometimes publish leading trade titles. The McGraw-Hill Book Co. and Prentice-Hall, Inc., business and professional publishers, have also been in the trade field for some time, Prentice-Hall with a regular trade de-partment, McGraw-Hill with an entire division of the cor-poration, Whittlesey House, occupied with trade business. The Macmillan Co. aims to publish virtually every kind of book; its current catalogues and its backlist of some 15,000 active titles are probably more varied than the lists of any other American publisher.

In recent years trade-book publishers have had a new competitor: the university presses.[5] Their place in trade publishing may be said to have been made official in June, 1944, when the *Saturday Review of Literature* issued its first University Press number. In 1945 *Publishers' Weekly* began its series of annual numbers on this subject. Long before this, of course, some university press books, normally sold direct by mail, were available in trade-book stores.

Trade publishing by university presses is a result of their wartime growth, the enterprise of certain of their managers, the fresh interest of university faculties in creative and popular writing, and most recently of the paradoxical effects of inflated publishing costs. As costs went up, especially for small editions, regular trade publishers became certain of sizable losses on serious books with limited market appeal and decided to abandon or avoid many such books. At the same time university presses, expecting to increase their profits, began to contract for them. Whether or not the profits materialized is debatable; the expectations arose because university presses, accustomed to sales in the hundreds, could think of trade books in the thousands; such books became available because regular trade publishers had begun to think in tens of thousands.

Generally speaking, university presses are neither as well endowed nor as heavily subsidized as some trade publishers, conscience-stricken over their rejections of serious books because of cost factors, like to believe. Most university presses pay no rent, but have somehow to meet all other business expenses. Normally most of their income comes from backlists of scholarly and scientific treatises. Datus Smith, Jr., director

[5]A full-scale "Survey of University Presses," with Chester Kerr as director, is in progress as this book goes to press. This survey was "sponsored by the American Council of Learned Societies through the Association of American University Presses with a grant from the Rockefeller Foundation." A comprehensive report is promised for the spring of 1949.

of the Princeton University Press, says that "the scholarly vigor of the whole backlist is of infinitely greater importance to the financial well-being of a press than the pyrotechnics, however beautiful, of a few current titles."[6]

Yet more and more university presses have begun to look to trade-book "pyrotechnics" for money with which to meet current bills for "saleless wonders." The extent of this movement is indicated in an article (which I was permitted to see in manuscript) prepared by Henry M. Silver for the spring, 1949, issue of the *American Scholar*. Silver compared the number of university press books reviewed in the Sunday New York *Times Book Review* "during the first six months of 1938 with the same period of 1948"; he found 33 books in the first period and 63 in the second. "In the earlier period only one press had six titles or more covered; in the latter, five. The 33 books of 1938 came from 12 presses; those of 1948 from 16. Of course only American university presses are here considered."

How many of these trade titles were profitable is not known; most of them, like most regular trade books, probably lost money. As Datus Smith, Jr., indicates, trade publishing by university presses, especially those least well off, is a risky policy; it becomes thrice risky when such presses, once successfully gambling, try to compete for trade merchandise with regular trade houses and even to outdo the latter in the quest for best sellers and book-club selections.[7]

[6]Letter to the author, August 20, 1948.

[7]In his article, "Dusting the Ivy Towers," in the *Saturday Review of Literature*, June 5, 1948, Datus Smith, Jr., says: "The university press that lowers standards 'to make money' will eventually lose its shirt. I know of no comprehensive set of figures to prove it, but I will bet that if you made a list of all the university press books that have paid out or broken even, the overwhelming majority of them would prove to be recognized works of scholarship; and that if you made another list consisting of those that had lost the most money, an impressive number of them would be those for which scholarly judgment had been to some extent tempered by commercial considerations, in the hope that they would be money-makers."

That university presses have done this is suggested by the publication and promotion by the University of Chicago Press a few years ago of Friedrich A. von Hayek's *The Road to Serfdom*, a sensational book previously rejected by at least one notable trade house which was quite aware of its sales possibilities. Further evidence is the publication by the Rutgers University Press of *The Lincoln Reader*, a Book-of-the-Month Club choice in February, 1947, but of only casual interest to scholars. Rutgers bought the two-page center spread in the *Publishers' Weekly*, May 8, 1948, to advertise to booksellers its new creation, *Gettysburg*, under the headline "Clues to a Bestseller." The advertisement hailed this as a "new and thrilling treatment of living history, fashioned with the remarkable technique that made THE LINCOLN READER a triumphant bestseller." "Remember," said the advertisement, "over 600,000 people visit the Battlefield of Gettysburg each year; 25,000,000 people now living have already been there."

Thus have university presses begun to turn to trade publishing, with its financial risks and editorial pitfalls. An opposite tendency may be noted among some newer trade houses, which, in order to balance the risks of trade publishing, have followed the lead of the oldest and most stable trade firms in publishing college textbooks or other bread-and-butter standbys with good backlist possibilities. An example is William Sloane Associates, a firm which started in 1947 with an ambitious and immediately successful trade list and the next year set up a college department under an experienced head. Earlier, Farrar, Straus & Co., organized in 1946, absorbed Hendricks House, a college textbook firm, which it now runs as a subsidiary. Alfred A. Knopf, Inc., Rinehart & Co., W. W. Norton & Co., the Bobbs-Merrill Co., notable names in trade publishing, all have college textbook lines. Rinehart also owns Murray Hill Books, Inc., which issues technical works; Duell, Sloan & Pearce owns Essential Books, a business and technical subsidiary. The passing in 1948 of one of the most promising trade-book houses, Reynal & Hitchcock, may be ascribed in some part to its failure to supplement its regular trade income: it tried without success a college department, a book club, and a pamphlet press.

TRADE PUBLISHING BY TRADE HOUSES   With some notable exceptions, the more or less purely trade publishing houses in America are the smaller ones. Those that do best usually have a specialty within the trade category—often a good juvenile list—and one or two star novelists: Wm. Morrow & Co. has Erle Stanley Gardner; Julian Messner, Inc., Frances Parkinson Keyes; the John Day Co., Pearl Buck; Coward-McCann, Inc., Elizabeth Goudge; Vanguard Press, James T. Farrell; Dial Press, Frank Yerby and Gladys Schmitt.

The exceptions are notable indeed. They include Doubleday & Co., Random House, Little Brown & Co., Viking Press, Simon & Schuster. Like the smaller trade houses, these firms look to star authors to quicken bookseller interest in their entire lists and maintain the sales volume essential to profitable operation. Established stars, however expensively promoted, sometimes fail; when they do, losses usually are high. That is the great risk in the star system. But that many star novelists can be depended upon to shine regularly is indicated by *Publishers' Weekly's* summary in the issue of January 24, 1948, of the twenty leading best sellers of 1947 (ten in fiction, ten in nonfiction). "In fiction," says the *Weekly*, "there is only one author who has not appeared before. In nonfiction, there is only one author, John Gunther, who has appeared before. . . . In fiction favorite authors repeat year after year."

At Doubleday much depends on stars like Thomas Costain, Kenneth Roberts, W. Somerset Maugham, Daphne du Maurier. Random House likes to see Sinclair Lewis in best seller form. Little, Brown looks to Samuel Shellabarger, A. J.

Cronin, John Marquand, James Hilton; Viking, to John Steinbeck and Upton Sinclair. At Simon & Schuster, where fiction has always been secondary, past stars have been Will Durant and Hendrik Willem Van Loon; more recently Dale Carnegie has shone, with *How to Win Friends and Influence People*, and his 1948 hit, *How to Stop Worrying and Start Living*. But Simon & Schuster's real stars are its editors, who come up year after year with "office-made" best sellers, such as *The Fireside Book of Folk Songs* and *A Treasury of Art Masterpieces*.

In any publishing season a star's book is likely to account for a sizable portion of his firm's gross income; this is true even of the large diversified firms whose trade departments also emphasize the star system. At Harper's, Betty Smith and Louis Bromfield, at Houghton Mifflin, Lloyd Douglas, and at Scribner's, Taylor Caldwell and Marcia Davenport hold star ratings. At Macmillan, Kathleen Winsor is a candidate for stardom. Sales of her first book, *Forever Amber*, accounted for about 10 percent of Macmillan's gross business in one year, including that from the firm's huge backlist and many special departments.

The purely trade-book houses are distinguished from the diversified firms by having no sizable textbook, technical, or other special business to share the overhead at all times and to succor the corporation when trade stars fail; the outstanding purely trade-book houses are distinguished from the smaller ones in that even when the former's stars fail, the firms may have successful trade-book seasons. Their losses on stars' books (like the losses of some of the diversified firms) are likely to be offset in varying degrees by profits from backlists of standard adult and juvenile titles; but their losses are likely to be offset, too, by profits from their own trade specialties, their own trade reprint lines, or their affiliated book clubs which sell trade titles.

Viking's Portable Library is a striking example of the ingenuity of a trade house without other lines in developing a trade specialty with long-term sales possibilities. Also outstanding is Simon & Schuster's merchandising of regular trade books in trade and special markets. This firm is largely responsible for the practice of issuing simultaneously cloth-bound and paper-bound editions of timely books, the paper-bound copies on the newsstands serving not only to achieve a large volume of sales for themselves but also as widely displayed advertisements for the longer lasting, higher-priced editions. Simon & Schuster has also made the most systematic use of reduced prepublication prices on costly gift books, thus building up large prepublication sales which make it safer to print in economical large editions. Another ingenious Simon & Schuster development is the Golden Books line of juveniles. This line is a big seller in regular bookstores, but is sold most widely outside them. Sometimes the Golden Books alone account for more than half of Simon & Schuster's annual total dollar volume.

The reprint holdings of the big purely trade houses include the Modern Library Books of Random House (indeed, Random House started as a reprint publisher) and Pocket Books in which Simon & Schuster is interested (both Simon & Schuster and Pocket Books are owned by Field Enterprises, Inc.). Doubleday's reprint subsidiary, Garden City Publishing Co., the largest hard-cover reprint house in the world, issues Blue Ribbon books, Sun Dial books, Star Dollar books, and other brands. Its newest line, designed to be sold on newsstands, is Permabooks, 35-cent hard-cover, nonfiction reprints of more expensive Garden City best sellers. In 1945 a syndicate including Little Brown, Random House, Harper's, Scribner's, and the Book-of-the-Month Club purchased Grosset & Dunlap, Inc., one of the big three in the hard-cover reprint field, along with Garden City and the World Publishing

Company, of Cleveland. Grosset & Dunlap and the Curtis Publishing Co. (owner of the *Saturday Evening Post*, the *Ladies Home Journal, Holiday*, and *Jack and Jill*) own shares of Bantam Books, which issues 25-cent paper-bound reprints.

In the book club field Doubleday again is dominant. It owns the Literary Guild, the largest of all in number of members, the huge Dollar Book Club, the Book League of America, three or four other adult clubs, the Junior Literary Guild, and the Young People's Division of the Literary Guild. Doubleday continues to try new reprint lines and new book clubs for special-subject and special-price markets. Its Mystery Guild, begun in January, 1949, distributes detective stories to members; its even newer Mutual Book Plan offers members a choice of 49-cent paper-bound books which have previously been best sellers in other Doubleday clubs. Partnership with the Book-of-the-Month Club in the Grosset deal may have brought Little Brown, Random House, Harper's, and Scribner's more snugly into the book-club orbit. Simon & Schuster was once a partner in Sears, Roebuck & Co.'s People's Book Club, but is no longer.

TRADE REPRINTERS AND BOOK CLUBS   Thus, unassociated with great trade-book firms there are but one major hard-cover reprint house, the World Publishing Co., and a few 25-cent paper-bound reprint houses, none of which approaches Pocket Books in size.

The outstanding independent publisher of paper-bound reprints is the formerly English affiliated Penguin-Pelican company, reorganized in 1948 as a wholly American firm: the New American Library of World Literature. Its publications are Signet (25-cent fiction) and Mentor (35-cent non-fiction) books. These and other paper-bound reprints are distributed, as are magazines, on newsstands, in drugstores, and at various other outlets; but the New American Library also cultivates most intensively the direct college and high-school markets and probably gets from them and from regular bookstores more of its volume of sales than does any other reprinter of paper-bound books. This is reflected in the New American Library's list, which is more serious and literary than those of other 25-cent houses, and in its policy, now almost unique among such houses, of keeping medium-sellers in print.

The New American Library, Pocket Books, and the Avon Book Company are the only important paper-bound firms not parts of periodical publishing houses. Bantam, as has been said, is partly owned by the Curtis Publishing Co. The Dell and Popular lines, each devoted almost exclusively to light fiction, are published by pulp magazine companies. One of the oldest, but smallest, of the better-known firms in the 25-cent field is American Mercury, Inc., which also issues the *American Mercury* magazine.

Among book clubs, the Book-of-the-Month Club, though partner with four trade publishers in the ownership of a reprint house, remains a giant independent. With this exception and possibly that of Sears, Roebuck's People's Book Club and the Greystone Corporation's Fiction Book Club, neither of which approaches the Book-of-the-Month Club or the big Doubleday subsidiaries in membership, sales, or dollar guarantees to trade publishers, there are only minor clubs. Their number fluctuates from week to week, but is estimated at about eighty. Of these, the Nonfiction Book Club and the Book Find Club are, perhaps, most prominent. The former, started in 1946 by Henry Holt & Co., was acquired early in 1948 by the Book-of-the-Month Club. The Greystone Corporation also plans to acquire other going clubs.

Each year, of course, each club selects fewer and less diversified titles than do most reprint houses. Yet the large number of clubs devoted to special subjects or special audiences tends to give book club titles some variety. Among the special subject clubs are the Natural History Book Club, Basic Books (medicine and psychology), the History Book Club, the Classics Club, and the National Travel Club; special-audience clubs are the Executive Book Club, the Negro Book Club, the Catholic Book Club, and clubs for children and adolescents.

These specialized clubs often can select titles not in demand by the giant clubs. The other minor independents sometimes have to settle for books passed over or rejected by competitors associated with a trade house, competitors who most often can also make original publishers more tempting cash offers. Independent reprinters, World and the unaffiliated paper-bound houses, also occasionally have difficulty in getting the titles they want, though here too the size of the cash offer is most often the determining factor. Also involved is the practice of original trade publishers of placing all the books of an author with the same reprint house, the aim being to give his second, third, and later books the advantage of long-range continuous promotion in the reprint market.

Major book club selections, whose sale to many thousands of club members sometimes appears to reduce the reprint market for them, are still pretty attractive reprint fare. In placing such books, cash offers once again are important, but here, too, the independent reprinter is sometimes shut out. Though there is said to be competitive bidding for them, Literary Guild (Doubleday) books almost uniformly go to Garden City (Doubleday) for hard-cover reprinting. The Book-of-the-Month Club–Grosset & Dunlap relationship, though close, has never developed this pattern; competitive bidding for Book-of-the-Month Club selections appears to result in the distribution of its titles among reprinters.

COMPETITION AMONG REGULAR PUBLISHERS   The advantages of affiliated hard-cover and paper-bound reprint houses and affiliated book clubs over most of the independents strengthen the affiliated publishers of originals in competition with independents in their own field. Such publishers are likely to be stronger still if they also have diversified nontrade lines. The key point is that publishing original trade books in America, especially adult books, has ordinarily been too shaky a business to stand firmly by itself. It has had to be supported by (1) textbook, technical book, business book or religious book publishing or (2) subsidiary trade activities, mainly the mass marketing at bargain prices of the small number of book club and reprint titles. Those firms that have compensated for their gamble on original trade books by either or both of these other types of business are now among the strongest firms in the trade-book industry. Others probably can compete successfully with them only by imitating them.

The result is that it has become continuously more expensive for new firms to gain footholds in the trade-book field and more difficult for older, essentially original-trade-book houses to survive without frequent best sellers and outside money from book clubs, reprinters, movie companies, digesters, or magazines. That a little of this outside money does fall to small independents is indicated by some 1948 book-club selections: Morrow had two Family Reading Club books and Messner one; Messner and Dial each had a Dollar Book Club title; the M. S. Mill Co. had a Book League choice, and the Westminster Press a People's Book Club and a Family Reading Club selection; John Day had a Literary Guild book. Yet, except for the Guild, these are all comparatively small-money clubs; in the competition for big club money the advantage naturally has been with big houses that have big trade lists. Between 1926 and 1948 twelve such houses accounted for 74 percent of Book-of-the-Month Club selections and a similar percentage of those of the Guild.[8]

[8]Doubleday; Viking; Houghton Mifflin; Rinehart; Harcourt, Brace; Little, Brown; Simon & Schuster; Macmillan; Harper's; Scribner's; Random House; and Knopf.

Though no one has carefully studied movie expenditures for books over a period of time, movie money has probably gone the same way as club money. In 1947 Metro-Goldwyn-Mayer made a deal with a small trade publisher, Farrar, Straus & Co., by which it agreed to share the cost of that company's elaborate scouting set-up in return for first look at scouts' manuscripts. But Farrar, Straus & Co. is an unusual small firm in that it is new, rich, and ambitious; as has been said, it has already taken on a textbook house. It is a firm on whose stability MGM can obviously count. Most other MGM deals have been made with big companies or their authors. It once agreed to pay half the salaries and traveling expenses of two Random House editors who scouted the nation for novels suited to MGM's needs; it advanced $100,000 to Carl Sandburg for screen rights to a novel, *Remembrance Rock*, published by Harcourt, Brace; it subsidized the advertising and production of Houghton Mifflin's MGM-novel-contest winner, *Raintree County*, so that it could be retailed at a lower price and thus become a more widely read advertisement for the movie.

Most newer or smaller trade-book enterprises have few such inducements to stay in business; they also suffer competitively in relations with literary agents, manufacturers, wholesalers, and many retailers.

THE OFFICIAL STATISTICS   One result of the combination of trade-book publishing with the publishing of textbooks, technical books, and other special lines and the integration of original trade houses with reprint companies and book clubs is the obfuscation of trade publishing statistics.

Though much quantitative information about book publishing is contained in the files of *Publishers' Weekly*, few efforts have been made to bring this information together in useful form. "The industry's statistics are practically nonexistent," said Cheney in 1931.[9] In 1947 Harry F. West, then managing director of the American Book Publishers' Council, found no improvement. He wrote: "It is not an exaggeration to state that book publishing is virtually the last important American industry which knows nothing of itself on a collective basis."[10] Council efforts to increase the industry's knowledge of itself resulted in useful statistical reports issued in October, 1947, and January, 1949, but even these do not give industry-wide pictures.[11] Differences in accounting practices rendered the data of some firms useless in general surveys; other firms showed the usual lack of interest and withheld their records; still others did not have in their own files, for their own use, the operating data requested.

Even gross industry-wide figures on annual dollar and copy volume are difficult to get in clear form. The figures that are available in divers census reports are only roughly comparable; even the definition of a "book" has frequently been altered.

On this matter the extended comment of *Bookbinding and Book Production*, the book manufacturers' trade journal, is illuminating. In its September, 1947, issue this journal said:

In the 1939 Census of Manufactures . . . the most comprehensive survey of bookbinding and book production yet made . . . plants whose products were less than $5,000 were not included. Maps, atlases, and globe covers were listed separately and not as books or pamphlets. No books or pamphlets published by federal, state, or city governments were included.

During the 1942-3 survey books were defined to include all collections of 32 pages or more. The production of smaller establishments and government plants was included.

In the present survey for 1945 all collections of 64 pages or more, and all hardbound editions irrespective of the number of

[9]Cheney, *Economic Survey of the Book Industry, 1930–1931*, p. 167.
[10]In a release on council activities, November 12, 1947.
[11]Some information from the 1947-48 Report appears in Appendix B.

pages, are considered books. Bluebooks, directories, catalogs, and the like, however, are excluded.

The conflicting definitions, which exist not only in official Census Reports but even in the industry itself and in the minds of plant officials who fill out these reports, do much to cast doubt upon the accuracy of final tabulations.

The census figures for 1945 are the most recent general ones, and these have faults besides those already noted. Most troublesome is the failure of the Census Bureau to distinguish book club sales from other mail order and subscription business, thus leaving the size of one of the then-fastest-growing parts of the book industry open to conjecture. How the bureau tabulated "originals" published by "reprint" houses also is obscure.

The census figures for 1945, nevertheless, are the best available.[12] They show that 1945 sales of all editions came to 428,832,884 copies, for which 1,080 publishers received $293,-360,380. On the basis of these totals some conclusions have been drawn about the degree of concentration in the book publishing industry. As the following table shows, "less than 3 percent of the book publishers in the United States [31 houses] put out more than 60 percent of the books sold," while 726 houses, "forming 67 percent of the total . . . published . . . less than 1 percent." The table is adapted from a bar chart in the September, 1947, issue of *Bookbinding and Book Production.*

Annual Sales Volume of All Publishers	Percentage of Publishers	Percentage of Books
$2.5 million and over	2.9	60.4
$500,000–$2,499,999	7.4	26.0
$250,000–$499,999	5.7	7.2
$50,000–$249,999	16.8	5.4
Under $50,000	67.2	1.0
TOTALS (=100 PERCENT)	1,080	428,832,884

[12]A summary, with other figures against which those for 1945 may be viewed, appears in Appendix B.

The census figures for 1945 show that trade books, in original and reprint editions (excluding those of book clubs), accounted for slightly more than 55 percent (in copies) of all book sales. About 44 percent of trade book sales were in the original editions, while of the remainder, 37 percent were hard-cover and 63 percent paper-bound reprints.

THE PRACTICAL STATISTICS   Though it issued a few warnings about the interpretation of the 1945 Census figures, the industry press boasted about the performance they disclosed. The boasts were justified, for 1945 was the industry's biggest year until then; yet the figures themselves, even were they wholly accurate, are somewhat unrealistic. The 1945 census report was not planned to give a statistical picture of the book publishing industry; it simply aimed to number the users of book paper. Many of those counted were not even nominally publishers, though for various purposes they may have printed or caused to be printed a number of "books." These "books" swell the number of titles and copies as well as that of "publishers," just as toy stores stocking occasional hobby or picture books or stationery stores carrying about thirty best-selling novels inflate the total of hard-cover book "outlets."

More realistic estimates of the total number of copies published by the book industry in 1945 and later years are not easily available. For the total number of firms in the industry a more meaningful figure than that of the census (1,080) is that reported annually in *Publishers' Weekly* for the number of houses that issued five or more titles the preceding year.[13] In six years, 1942–47, this figure ranged from 222 in 1944 to 299

[13]A somewhat larger figure is suggested by the American Booksellers Association's 1947–48 *Book Buyer's Handbook*, which, striving for completeness, listed the discount and returns policies of the 266 publishers who had issued five or more titles in 1946 and of other houses added at the request of certain booksellers. The grand total was "338 publishing imprints," a few of which were wholly owned subsidiaries of firms listed separately. The 1948–49 *Handbook* listed 362 "publishing imprints."

in 1947; a fair average is 250 firms. This figure includes publishers of reprints as well as publishers of originals of all kinds; it is probably comprehensive enough for any description of the actual book publishing industry. A smaller, but probably even more practical, figure is that for the membership of the American Book Publishers Council; in 1948 the council had about ninety members, including virtually without exception the foremost trade publishing houses as well as a majority of the sizable college textbook, technical, and other specialized publishers.

In the original trade book field the thirty-two firms already mentioned in this narrative and a few others, including Dodd, Mead & Co., E. P. Dutton & Co., G. P. Putnam's Sons, the Thomas Y. Crowell Co., the Creative Age Press, and New Directions, account for the great bulk of the business. A few specialty houses, such as A. S. Barnes & Co. for sport books, Greenberg Publisher for self-help items, William R. Scott, Inc., and Holiday House, Inc., for juveniles, may be added. This makes forty-two companies. Perhaps twelve university presses should also be counted, making the total fifty-four.

One of the leading New York literary agents uses a list of twenty-eight first-run companies and fifteen supplementary ones; he has submitted manuscripts to few others. In recent years fifty-five publishers have offered books to the Literary Guild; the Book-of-the-Month Club, with more frequent nonfiction choices than the Guild, has had books from a few more.

The 1948 *Literary Market Place*, an authorative publishing-industry directory issued annually by R. R. Bowker & Co., the owner of *Publishers' Weekly*, lists sixty-six original trade-book houses "whose travellers regularly visit the bookstores throughout the country." These sixty-six trade-book houses include: 21 of the 91 school and college textbook publishers listed in this directory; 10 of the 65 technical and business publishers; 11 of the 59 religious publishers; 6 of the 13 Bible publishers; and 9 of the 25 medical publishers.

Comparable statistics on carefully selected subjects from each of these sixty-six trade-book houses would give all of them much valuable information on the original trade-book publishing industry. The reprint industry, had it comparable data on the three big hard-cover and the seven paper-bound publishers mentioned in this chapter, would also be well informed about itself. The book club picture is complicated by the great number of new clubs, but full information about Doubleday's enterprises, the Book-of-the-Month Club, the People's Book Club, and the Fiction Book Club would be useful.

The American Book Publishers Council is making progress in its efforts to improve the industry's statistics. Similar efforts are being made by other trade associations, among them the American Booksellers Association, the Book Manufacturers Institute, the American Text Book Publishers Institute, and the Association of American University Presses. Already each branch of the book industry represented by these associations has a better understanding of its own operations than it had five years ago. This self-knowledge will become even greater as industry record keeping improves and fuller statistical reports from more and more firms become available.

The next step, then, must be to attempt strictly to assay the relations among the various parts of the book publishing industry. These parts, as the evidence in this chapter indicates, have always been more interdependent, perhaps, than industry leaders themselves have realized. They are likely to become more interdependent still as investments in publishing companies become larger and the risks in each part of the industry increase. This interdependence will be manifest, if present tendencies continue, not only among publishing firms, but among the various departments of individual houses, especially the newly integrated ones. One of the major events of the 1947 publishing season was the merger of D. Appleton-Century with F. S. Crofts & Co. Early the following year Reynal & Hitchcock combined with Harcourt, Brace & Co. Other mergers have occurred in recent months. Commenting on the industry as a whole the Sunday New York *Times Book Review* said on December 19, 1948:

The new year will probably see a series of marriages in the trade, and perhaps on other grounds as well a decrease in the number of individual American publishers. It seems to be a fact that fewer substantial new publishing firms set up shop in 1948 than in any other recent year, and that conditions dictate further concentration rather than expansion.

2

THE CHANGING EDITORIAL ENVIRONMENT

AMONG HIGHBROWS, trade publishers are commonly looked upon as businessmen trafficking in books; among lowbrows, as bookish men in business. Most publishers are resigned to being damned in both camps; they know they can often do best with serious works by promoting them as merchandise, that they can maximize profits on some merchandise by treating it as serious work.[1]

Many trade publishers believe that profits in recent years have come mainly from merchandise sold outside the bookstore market, and they make and promote their lists accordingly. Though they issue proportionately less fiction now than they did before the war, more of it is selected as bait for big book club and movie offers and bids from reprinters, digesters, and occasionally from popular magazines. When a publisher contracts for fiction unsuited to these agencies, it may be that for him literature comes first; but probably he is also cultivating willing young authors for later subsidiary markets.

Even publishers who have not had much luck in these markets continue to be tempted by the few rich plums dangling there; the often reckless competition for them is justified by the recent public statements of some industry leaders concerning the poverty of the older trade. Typical of such state-

[1]"Merchandise" is not the author's word, but one in common use in the industry. Some publishers require their editors to classify recommended manuscripts as "serious" or "merchandise."

ments is that of the late Alfred R. McIntyre, president of Little, Brown, who said in the *Atlantic*, October, 1947, that his company "will depend for its profit from its trade department [in 1947] almost entirely on its special income . . . from book club adoptions, royalties on the leasing of plates for cheap editions, and revenue from the sale of other subsidiary rights." Bennett Cerf, president of Random House, said in his regular column in the *Saturday Review of Literature*, June 5, 1948, that trade publishers must "depend more and more on subsidiary rights . . . to show profits, or even to meet the overhead." Cass Canfield, board chairman of Harper's, and Lovell Thompson, vice president of Houghton Mifflin, have echoed these pronouncements.

One hesitates to gainsay such authorities or the records upon which their statements presumably are based. Yet the accounting records of most regular trade publishers are usually so kept that they distort the modern income and profit picture; they make one challenge the validity of statements based on them and the soundness of the resulting policies.

As in the period preceding the great expansion of book club, reprint, and other subsidiary markets, so today, in most houses, all of a trade publisher's promotion and manufacturing expenditures on a book and also a share of the general overhead continue to be charged to the book's account, while this account is credited only with the revenue from the sale of the book to bookstores, wholesalers, and libraries. Thus, a novel may be promoted at great expense to whet the interest of subsidiary markets or to compensate clubs and movies for prepublication commitments, and it may be manufactured in a costly big edition to justify the promotion outlay. If this novel then does not become a best seller in the stores, it appears on the publisher's records and usually in his mind as a costly failure. This is true even if the book becomes a big club selection or a reprint and if the publisher shares in movie, digest, or serial money earned by it, for all such income usually is credited to a separate account, "income from the sale of subsidiary rights."

Ordinarily there is no separate account for the costs of earning this income or entailed in the pursuit of it; revenue from the sale of subsidiary rights appears entirely as profit and looks excellent on the books. Revenue from bookstore or library sales, on the other hand, is offset by all the costs and thus usually looks very poor. Moreover, the actual gross revenue from bookstores may be adversely affected by their having to sell, at high prices set by the publisher and fixed by law for bookstore sale, merchandise originally selected and expensively promoted for distribution through the subsidiary and often cut-rate channels.

Thus, publishing for subsidiary markets is not necessarily as good business as it is sometimes made to appear. The possible editorial consequences, in turn, give pause even to publishers proud of reaching the huge subsidiary audiences. Lovell Thompson, for example, wrote in the *Saturday Review of Literature*, March 1, 1947:

The American book particularly, represents the freest free press there is and the freest, most open intellectual experiment. . . . That is what has made the book industry a laboratory of public taste—a laboratory used and paid for by the movie, the reprinter, the digester, and in less degree by the radio and even by the magazines.

But the publishing of a book, Thompson continued,

must remain a small operation, else the publisher will publish what all think is fair instead of what he thinks is good. . . . It is important to maintain his interest in his channels to media such as movies and big circulation magazines, which are less free, more money-bound or more subscriber-bound than he. On the other hand, it is important to keep him independent of these media.

Literary critics often have denounced trade publishers for their failure to heed this caveat; and even daily book reviewers, convinced that most publishers are already too keenly aware of easy book club, movie, or reprint money, occasionally refer to books produced for subsidiary markets as "fat 'historical' tripe."[2] Bookstore salespeople who have to sell this "tripe" to their customers face to face also complain; as witness, Miss Lillian Friedman, head of the book department of Stix, Baer & Fuller in St. Louis. Of book clubs she says (italics mine): "In the main they choose and foist upon the public and *stimulate publishers into seeking among their manuscripts* over-long, over-padded historical novels . . . full of everything but real situations and real people."[3]

But after all it is a truism that if publishers view subsidiary markets as the ones in which most and quickest profits can be made, as businessmen they will produce books for these markets. That they do this is scarcely news, nor is it news that this practice has its critics.

Yet something new is happening in trade publishing, akin, perhaps, to what happened years ago in the movies and in radio, when distributors such as Marcus Loew (MGM), Barney Balaban (Paramount), and Spyros Skouras (Twentieth Century-Fox) and salesmen such as Niles Trammel (NBC), Mark Woods (ABC), and Edgar Kobak (Mutual) took over the essentially editorial functions.[4] What is new in trade publishing is not that in selecting and editing books the publishers are keeping both eyes on what appear to be the biggest and

[2]New York *Herald Tribune*, January 27, 1948. See also William McFee in the New York *Sun*, December 1, 1948.

[3]*Publishers' Weekly*, January 31, 1948.

[4]On radio see John Crosby, "Radio and Who Makes It," the *Atlantic*, for January, 1948; on the movies see Ruth A. Inglis, *Freedom of the Movies*, Chicago, University of Chicago Press, 1947; Mae D. Huettig, *Economic Control of the Motion Picture Industry; a Study in Industrial Organization*, Philadelphia, University of Pennsylvania Press, 1944.

surest markets, but that the marketers are beginning to select and to censor books for the publishers.

A MODERN EDITOR'S DUTY   One of the probable roots of this revolution in trade publishing lies in the changing nature of the large American publishing houses themselves and reflects that diversification and expansion of their activities, mentioned above. Ken McCormick, editor-in-chief of Doubleday's trade department, recently described the emerging situation.

The most important change in an editor's job today [he said in the 1948 Bowker Lecture] is that he has slowly acquired the publisher's responsibility. This is particularly true in the United States. In England, the head of the house, the publisher, still chooses his own list, keeps track of all authors, and gives little credit to others. Editors and readers are seen but not heard. In the United States, editors have come to know a sort of new freedom in which editorial decisions are more and more in their hands.

Then McCormick put his finger on the reason for this: "The publisher," he said, "now concerns himself far more than ever before with business management."[5]

In publishing houses, as in other modern corporations, business managers can best administer their affairs in business or financial terms. These are not new to the book industry; they have always formed part of the vocabulary of financially successful publishers. As more American houses become big and bureaucratized, however, financial terms tend to be the only ones different departments are likely to retain in common;

[5]The Richard Rogers Bowker Memorial Lectures, in remembrance of the former owner and editor of *Publishers' Weekly*, have been given annually since 1938 at the New York Public Library by leading publishers, editors, and authors, and published by the library. Ken McCormick's is called *Editors Today;* the quotations on the succeeding pages are also from it. See also the remarks of Spencer Curtis Brown, head of the Curtis Brown literary agency in London and long acquainted with publishing on both sides of the Atlantic, in *Publishers' Weekly*, December 6, 1947.

they thus tend to become the basic language of the firm. In big companies, company-wide policy can only be made in such language, and values that cannot adequately be discussed in it tend to atrophy and their influence to diminish. Only in financial terms can the publisher measure one department's performance against that of the others; only thus can he estimate the contributions of each to the whole enterprise. Consequently financial reports tend to usurp the major lines of contact between modern publishers and their editors, of whom the original trade editor is but one, and the latter's work, as well as the performance of his authors, come increasingly to be judged by their financial showing.

McCormick made this new situation explicit when he said:

Maxwell Perkins [the late, brilliant editor at Scribner's] took the position that an editor had no interest in anything but the book itself; that his responsibility lay solely with the author and that once he had discharged that responsibility his part of the work ceased. For the generation to which he belonged he was right; but the fact remains that publishing is not that simple today. Editors must have some business sense, which should be directed to the benefit of the author and the publisher alike.

Under these circumstances, however independent the editor personally may be, he is less likely than the owner-publisher himself to risk failure on a literary experiment or a hunch. This is especially true in periods of narrow profit margins and declining sales, when, whatever his editorial judgment, an editor's doubt about the financial merit of a book or an author may prompt him to censor or to abandon both. Then, also, an editor is less likely to compromise his firm and his job in the opposite way: by passing over reasonably sure financial coups. How pleasant, then, to have a friendly movie company or magazine, or a neighborly book club or reprinter, or a newfangled market expert, offer a promising manuscript or an idea for one, especially when subsidies for promotion and manufacturing are part of the package.

To quote McCormick again (italics mine):

> The Metro-Goldwyn-Mayer novel contest was the first overt act which indicated that movie companies realized the part publishers play in making a book attractive as a movie to the public. This contest has been followed by numerous tie-ups in which *editors have been encouraged to accept movie money to help finance the writing of novels.* This can hardly be called an evil but it is a new temptation toward a short cut to big sales.

Not that the publisher himself, nowadays, is likely to scrutinize gift horses too closely. Moreover, it is easier for him to rationalize his own cupidity when underlings take the profit-making short cuts. This being so, it becomes easier still for ambitious underlings to welcome apparently sure-profit merchandise from modern marketers.

THE MODERN READER'S TASTE   But that is only the root of the matter in the publishing house itself. Outside and increasingly urgent are the modern markets' peculiar needs.

Long before these markets grew to their present size, trade publishers often were criticized for not spending money for market research. R. L. Duffus spoke for many critics when he said in 1930:

> Studies of consumers' interests are being constantly made, at great expense, by advertisers and advertising agencies, and sometimes by magazines and newspapers. Authors and publishers must do the same. It becomes more and more obvious that, except in the case of creative literature, the book must be adjusted to its probable readers, and adjusted on a surer basis of knowledge about those readers than now exists. I am not even sure that creative literature need be excepted.[6]

[6]R. L. Duffus, *Books; Their Place in a Democracy*, Boston, Houghton, 1930, p. 219.

As book club, reprint, digest, and movie markets grew larger and the risk involved in publishing for them increased, Duffus' old advice must have become more pertinent. Yet until the wartime boom very few publishers of original trade books heeded it, and the results of the few market-research projects since attempted have for good reasons been skeptically received.[7] Market experts still are unable to forecast the sales of individual books with anything like the accuracy they achieve with soup, soap, or cosmetics. Most of the techniques for book market research remain in an experimental stage; moreover, the usable ones are costly and time consuming. Few small publishers can afford the cost; no publisher with a sizable list each season can afford the time to test more than a few items.

Most trade publishers, therefore, have been content to watch closely the results of the book market research undertaken from time to time by the marketers who most need and can best afford it—the richer book clubs, the reprinters, and the movie companies. So far, their research seems to confirm the belief that as the new markets have grown, the range of emotions and ideas acceptable to the mass of their patrons has shrunk. The markets' requirements seem thus to have become more specialized, though, paradoxically, the best way to meet them seems to be with least specialized books.

This, too, presents revolutionary problems to the American trade publishing industry, which, whatever its recent deep and foreshadowing changes, is still geared to a limited market for the publishers' or editors' private choices. The modern marketers' difficulty is that the nature of publishers' choices

---

[7]One of the most ambitious of these is also one of the poorest, though sponsored by the book industry and done at great cost. This is Link and Hopf, *People and Books; a Study of Reading and Book-Buying Habits.* For an excellent review of this work by Dean Bernard Berelson of the Graduate Library School, University of Chicago, see the *Library Quarterly,* January, 1947, pp. 71–73.

has changed more slowly than the markets themselves; the revolutionary solution is for reprinters, book clubs, and particularly movie companies to undertake to supplement the publishers' lists with choices of their own—choices that seem to have to borrow distinction or other selling points by first appearing as original trade books.

To lend marketers' manuscripts distinction, to "famous them up," as one publishing executive put it, or otherwise to improve their chances in the subsidiary markets has become a new role of the publisher of original books—a role that he has not yet played very often, at least overtly, yet one that he may grace more frequently as integration with outside agencies becomes more common.

REPRINTERS' NEEDS   Probably least aggressive in urging this new role upon the publishers have been the reprint houses, especially the hard-cover reprinters who distribute their own self-help books, anthologies, juveniles, and other originals mainly in markets used by the regular trade firms. These reprinters also do well in regular book outlets with regular trade best sellers and book club and movie selections—marked down.

Most paper-bound reprinters, in turn, also are successful with leading regular trade titles in the magazine markets. These reprinters, moreover, do much of their business in detective stories, westerns, and light romances, sex appeal (to judge by many titles and covers and sometimes by the contents) being the common basis upon which they compete among themselves and with the mass magazines for display space on newsstands. That the majority of the readers of these books are not expected to respond to preliminary, prestige-laden promotion by original trade publishers is indicated by the reprinters' practice, often at the suggestion of market analysts, of changing the titles of hard-cover originals. This practice traps some readers of original books into buying reprints in their new guise, but it also attracts many buyers who ordinarily do not read books at all. Were it not for the type of book usually involved, title changes that result in thousands of new readers might be justified as a way culturally to improve the breed. But typical is Eric Hatch's *Five Days* metamorphosed by Bantam into *Five Nights*, one change that conveys the intent of all.[8]

The very success in the 25-cent market of detective stories, westerns, and light romances, however, has so reduced their sales at hard-cover prices that some of their best creators, rather than depend on low reprint royalties that must be shared with regular publishers, have turned to other kinds of writing. Thus, most paper-bound publishers, as their markets expand, find it increasingly difficult to keep their newsstand space filled with satisfactory reprints of this type. Their predicament is worsened by a growing marketing practice. These publishers now issue most of their books as "one shots"; at more or less regular intervals they make one huge printing of a title (seldom less than 150,000 copies), distribute it like a single issue of a magazine (often with sizable returns, many of which are pulped) and then follow it by a similar but new book. They do no new printings unless the market seems to warrant a whole new issue of a title, which is then handled again like a new issue of a magazine. The returns problem keeps all 25-cent publishers in the backlist business, which they solicit chiefly in the school market. Of the major paperbound reprinters only the New American Library keys an appreciable part of its list to such business. The other paper-

[8]There was once some expectation that 25-cent books, by making a host of new readers, would eventually enlarge the market for serious new books, but this has now been dissipated. It is probable that the huge wartime Armed Services Editions have been similarly disappointing. For a useful statement of their history and a list of all the titles see *Editions for the Armed Services, Inc.*, published by the Editions, New York, 1948, especially pp. 17–21.

bound reprinters simply use up more and more titles in their small subject range.

Some paper-bound reprinters have always issued original anthologies, cookbooks, and the like; the growing scarcity of usable fiction has recently forced them to plan originals in that and related fields. According to the *Writers' Journal*, June, 1948, Pocket Books planned "an experiment with original fiction, and if the innovation is successful a dying market for [writers of] book-length westerns and light love stories will be revived." Bantam's plans include a "new kind of book-and-film tie-in to consist of books designed to give movie fans, in highly readable form, the authentic record of historic events around which the film stories are constructed." Its first "tie-in" book, said *Publishers' Weekly*, July 31, 1948, was *Joan of Arc*, by Frances Winwar,

a revised version of the author's *The Saint and The Devil*, rewritten with omissions and substitutions to parallel the story of the Ingrid Bergman RKO movie which is based on Maxwell Anderson's play, *Joan of Lorraine*. . . . Similar books in the program are being planned. Some of them may be brand new books, especially commissioned for the purpose. Some may be revisions of lively books already in existence.

The New American Library has published two original novels, *No Pockets in a Shroud*, by Horace McCoy, previously issued abroad, but not in the United States, and *Kiss of Death*, by Eleazar Lipsky, adapted from the author's shooting script for the movie of the same name. Convinced that paper-bound reprinters, on their own, can make valuable additions to the serious reading fare of the nation, especially of the schools, the editors of the New American Library are planning other originals for their Mentor (nonfiction) list.

Yet one of the best selling points of paper-bound books is believed to be the bargain appeal of "complete and unabridged" $2.50–$4.00 items for 25 or 35 cents. Thus, while reprinters are venturing on independent original publishing, some of them are wary of it. Also wary are the regular trade publishers themselves, who see the obvious threat here to their reprint royalties. Indeed, complaints from these publishers are thought to have caused Pocket Books to slow down its program of original fiction and may have deterred others even from planning such programs. A businesslike solution, parallel to *Reader's Digest* "plants" which subsequently appear in the *Digest* as coming from magazines accepting them, may be prior or simultaneous publication of reprinters' originals by regular trade publishers.

Certain nonfiction books, in fact, have already been handled in this way, additional motives in some instances being the reprinter's wish to give the authors a chance at regular trade royalties and to give public and private libraries an opportunity to acquire lasting hard-cover editions. Pocket Books initiated and shared composition and other costs with Coward-McCann on an anthology of humorous verse by David McCord, the original edition appearing approximately a year earlier than the "reprint." A similar arrangement, though somewhat different in details, was made between Pocket Books and Duell, Sloan & Pearce for the publication of Dr. Benjamin Spock's *Book of Baby and Child Care*, issued by the "original" publisher some months before the Pocket edition appeared. The New American Library also has sold at least two nonfiction originals for prior hard-cover publication: *America in Perspective*, edited by Henry Steele Commager, to Random House, and *Indians of North America*, by John Collier, to Norton.

Given such precedents, the paper-bound publishers' dictum "we always want a reprint," these publishers' persistent and worsening shortage of salable fiction, and the original publishers' practice of "famousing up" fiction for the movie companies—given these conditions, it hardly seems farfetched to believe that publishers of originals would "value up" fiction for the cheap reprinters from whom the long-run cash returns are likely to be greater and more direct than from the movie companies and with whom, in certain instances, publishers of originals are more closely associated. At least one "original" publisher has already shown his willingness to conform to reprinters' needs by consulting on editorial matters relating to the manuscript of a second novel the paper-bound publisher who had reprinted the author's first novel.

Regular publishers might look even more favorably on fiction from reprinters if on such books they were to share in royalties from book clubs, such as Doubleday's new Mystery Guild, which is aiming at monthly sales of 100,000 hardbound copies of detective stories. The success of this club may also help solve the problem of detective story *author's* royalties which, appreciably enlarged, would then come mainly from the hard-cover sale.

As for royalties on other 25-cent original fiction, novelist James T. Farrell, who follows the publishing industry closely and has written provocatively about it, can see ahead to the time when "authors are hired by reprint houses as they are now by Hollywood."[9] Book industry prototypes are the salaried writers who turned out the old boy's book series,[10] and the artists and writers who for fees and no royalties on sales create many of today's juveniles.

NEEDS OF THE CLUBS   Some book clubs with more homogeneous memberships than the Book-of-the-Month Club believe that they can reduce the wants of their members to a formula, but like the reprinters of paper-bound books, they are not

[9]James T. Farrell, *The Fate of Writing in America*, New York, New Directions, 1945, p. 23; this pamphlet is reprinted in his *Literature and Morality*. Lovell Thompson, in the *Saturday Review of Literature*, March 1, 1947, also refers to the "time when the reprinter can buy his own potboilers."

[10]An illuminating article is "Boys' Books," *Fortune*, April, 1934.

certain that they can get authors to write satisfactory formula books. One such club is the People's Book Club, part of whose formula was stated in its advertisement on the back cover of Sears, Roebuck's 1948 *Spring and Summer Catalogue:*

The standards by which our editors and critics judge literature contain this one very vital *must:* The books must be readable by every member of the family. They must be *family books.* . . . So if you like to read without blushing, without tearing pages out before passing the book on to the younger members of your household, we invite you . . . to read about the advantages you will enjoy as a member of the People's Book Club.

Neither the Literary Guild nor the Book-of-the-Month Club applies such standards. John Beecroft, who alone selects Literary Guild books and those for most other Doubleday clubs (from short lists passed on by corps of readers), could probably say what the formula for a Guild success is; if he did he would surely rate plot and suspense above purity, though he might caution a writer not to attempt to achieve in fact the image of prurience and passion so familiar in the Guild's advertisements.

The Book-of-the-Month Club offers its members each year a greater variety of selections than any other club, with the possible exception of the Book Find Club. But even Book-of-the-Month Club selections are not different enough one from another to support the allegation of Harry Scherman, the club's founder and president, that they are in fields "quite as wide as current literature" and thus cannot be typed.[11]

Scherman, his fellow executives, and indeed the five eminent literary figures themselves who as the club's board of judges make the club's selections, assert that this board chooses from the whole range of new trade books each year only those it thinks best—not best for the club or its members,

[11]On the general nature of Book-of-the-Month Club choices see Merle Miller, "The Book Club Controversy," *Harper's*, June, 1948, especially p. 521.

but best according to its own taste.[12] This presumably reflects the highest literary standards and is the club's guarantee of range and quality to readers uncertain of their ability to select the best for themselves.

Because of management's wish, however, that selections be made by unanimous vote—a result believed by at least one of the board to be the goal of democratic process[13]—some of the judges must from time to time relax their own standards in order for them all to concur. This not only must limit the range of club selections, for the area of forced agreement can only be part of the whole available field, but it must also render them—for some of the judges perhaps all the time and all the judges some of the time—representative of their second or third best, not their most lofty standards. Indeed, since Book-of-the-Month Club management, in the persons of Scherman and Vice-President Meredith Wood, retains the privilege of adding titles to the small group from which the board ultimately makes its selection each month, the selections may

[12]In her 1947 Bowker Lecture, *Book Clubs* (New York, New York Public Library, 1947), Book-of-the-Month Club judge Dorothy Canfield Fisher says (p. 22): "From the very first meeting, we were told by Mr. Scherman and Mr. Haas, then a partner, now at Random House, that what was asked of us literary people, was a purely literary effort. We were to put our heads together to try to agree on which book of all of those we had read in the month preceding the meeting, we had liked and enjoyed most. We were not to try to guess which book the reading public would like—because that has proved to be a sphinx-question to which no Oedipus has ever found the answer. But here we were, five very differing American readers, with all kinds of special interests, with widely differing personalities. If there were some book or books which struck us all as superior to the others, there was a reasonable chance that the book would strike other readers as superior."
On this theme see also the autobiography of another club judge: Henry S. Canby, *American Memoir*, Boston, Houghton, 1947, p. 361; and Merle Miller, "The Book Club Controversy," *Harper's*, June, 1948, p. 521.

[13]See Dorothy Canfield Fisher, *Book Clubs*, p. 38: "Another variety of book club is now operating which might be called the totalitarian variety, in that the books are chosen by one person." But surely this businesslike locating of responsibility in one person is no more "totalitarian" than the unanimity of a cabal.

often be representative, not so much of the board's standards as of management's idea, nurtured on the findings of market analysts, of what club members themselves want.

The club's judges are well paid not only in salary but in bonuses and awards under a profit sharing plan. For the year 1946 none received less than $22,476, and one got $25,933. Simply out of regard for the revenue that makes such remuneration feasible, it would seem that these judges would keep the wants of the members, as reflected in past sales, in mind. That they probably do so, sometimes knowingly in defiance of their own standards (the alternative is that they are extraordinarily eccentric even for literary people) is suggested by some statistics assembled by Joseph Margolies, vice-president of Brentano's, Inc.

At a PEN Club dinner late in 1947, Margolies said that as a Book-of-the-Month Club subscriber he had compared the selections offered that year by the club with books chosen in December, 1947, by 126 literary critics and others active in literary and scholarly work. These people listed their selections in one of three journals: the *New Republic*, the New York *Herald Tribune* (under the head "Books I Have Liked"), or the New York *Times*, where twelve of them named the "ten they consider 'best'—or anyhow outstanding —in 1947." All told, 496 books were listed. Margolies was surprised to find that among them were only four of the seventeen (including dual selections) books-of-the-month for the year (only one Literary Guild book was named). Dorothy Canfield Fisher, a Book-of-the-Month Club judge, in listing three 1947 titles in the New York *Herald Tribune*, mentioned only one of the seventeen BOMC selections; another judge, Clifton Fadiman, did not mention any.[14]

Besides putting books on the final list from which selections

[14]This showing, among the critics, of Book-of-the-Month Club selections must have been discouraging to Judge Henry Seidel Canby, who wrote in

are made, in 1947 BOMC management began to offer members alternate selections not made by the judges.[15] For a time the club offered between 70 and 100 alternate titles with full membership credit, but because of opposition from bookstores and some publishers, and probably because this procedure detracted from the focussed appeal of the single (or dual) book(s)-of-the-month, the offer has been greatly curtailed. Now, if the judges choose a nonfiction title, management may offer a novel on the same terms.

An incident that occurred late in 1947 also shows management consideration for some of the club's members. The board of judges had selected for January, 1948, distribution the MGM prize novel *Raintree County*, by Ross Lockridge, Jr., published by Houghton Mifflin. The selection was denounced by a Jesuit spokesman for the Roman Catholic Church. According to the New York *Times*, February 19, 1948, "in the edition being sent by the club to its subscribers, one sentence that was regarded objectionable from a religious viewpoint has been removed," presumably with the consent of the author, the publisher, and the movie company.

Earlier, because "MGM thought it would sell more copies if it were shorter" (the words are those of the novelist's wife), Lockridge literally exhausted himself in working over *Raintree County*. The Book-of-the-Month Club, obviously not for the first time in its history, also had made suggestions, accepted by author and publisher, for tailoring the book to club needs. Of this Dorothy Canfield Fisher said: Lockridge's "reaction to suggestions from the Committee of

his *American Memoir*, pp. 360–61: "The teacher of literature seldom knows how effective (or ineffective) his teaching has been until years have matured his students and settled their patterns of life. We [at the club] could test our success and failures in a few months. Not, let me hasten to add, by the sales figures of the books we sent out. . . . What counted for success in our eyes was the impression made upon critics and readers, the impact of the book, which was easy enough to register."

[15]This plan is discussed in Dorothy Canfield Fisher, *Book Clubs*, pp. 37–38.

Selection of the Book-of-the-Month Club was mature, not self-willed, not stubborn, very reasonable and intelligent, rather unusual with a young and untried author."[16]

Though publishers overload their lists each year with candidates for club selection, the clubs, as do the paper-bound reprinters, still have difficulty, even after meddling with contents and titles, in finding enough books suited to their members' wants. As yet, however, again like the reprinters, they have made only tentative approaches to this problem. Perhaps even more than reprints, club selections, which often are manufactured to ape trade editions in appearance, seem to need trade prestige. Trade publication also makes them obvious bargains, Book-of-the-Month Club books often and those of other big clubs always being offered at prices well below what the bookstores must charge. Bookstore prices also give tone to club gifts, dividends, and bonuses; the Book-of-the-Month Club, for example, advertised late in 1948 that "in the past two years, over $30,000,000 worth of books (retail value) were distributed free among the Club's members."[17]

For these reasons most clubs are reluctant to try to sell their own originals. They are deterred also by the expected opposition of regular publishers, who are still the sovereign source of club titles and even more alert to threats to their shares of book club royalties than of reprint royalties. Some of the smaller clubs like the Executive Book Club and Our

---

[16]Nanette Kutner, "Ross Lockridge, Jr.—Escape from Main Street," *Saturday Review of Literature*, June 12, 1948. This extraordinarily perceptive article, published soon after Lockridge had committed suicide, tells of the grasp of commercialism and its agencies on one confused young American writer.

[17]For 1947 alone the retail value of the club's free books was $16 million, which *Publishers' Weekly*, November 27, 1948, compared to the $6 million "in merchandise and cash" which "radio programs have been reported to have given away" that year. But more interesting is the fact, noted by *Publishers' Weekly*, that the $16 million in free books actually cost the Book-of-the-Month Club less than $2,500,000.

Book Club, Inc., however, talk of "commissioning writers to prepare" nonfiction selections, and among the larger ones, Sears' People's Book Club has already issued, independently, at least five "gift" books.

Perhaps most significant are the precedents established by the major clubs, especially the Book-of-the-Month Club, by which club and publisher can eat their cake and have it too. As with reprints, these precedents involve prior or simultaneous publication by regular publishers of originals specially fashioned to the established wants of club members. So far this practice, too, has been limited to free books. One such was the December, 1947–January, 1948, Book-of-the-Month Club dividend, *A Treasury of Short Stories*, edited by Bernardine Kielty, wife of Harry Scherman and columnist for the Book-of-the-Month Club *News*. It was published by Simon & Schuster. Another was the October–November, 1947, Book-of-the-Month Club dividend, *Favorite Poems of Henry Wadsworth Longfellow*, edited by Henry Seidel Canby, chairman of the club's board of judges. This was published by Doubleday.

Many clubs and publishers deny that fiction can be written to order, though the People's Book Club's success with the Sindlinger-North novel *So Dear to My Heart*[18] and other clubs' tailoring of existing manuscripts for the club market would seem to weaken their stand. Moreover, every magazine fiction editor knows that novels have been written to specifications and that some of them, first serialized in mass periodicals, have appeared later on regular publishers' lists and, indeed, as major book club choices.

Some novelists themselves who have been enriched by club money also seem to know the formula. The testimony of one of them, F. van Wyck Mason, is germane. Mason, a former pulp writer who, according to an interview printed in *Cosmo-*

[18]See below, pp. 49–50.

politan, July, 1948, "has turned out thirty-three books in twenty years, with a total sale of twenty-two million copies," many of them distributed by major book clubs, says of his work:

A writer who knows his business can turn out any kind of story you want. . . . Here is my picture of myself as a writer, reduced to simplest terms. I'm a cave man. You and your family are in your cave just starting a meal. I come along, hungry, wanting some of that meal. I haven't done any hunting, I haven't done any fishing, but if you'll give me some food I'll tell you a story and take your mind off your troubles. That's our contract. You say okay and give me some meat. Now what should I do? Should I tell you a story that I think will please and interest and thrill you? Of course I should! That was the basis of our bargain. You didn't bargain to be a sounding board while I talked to please myself and make a reputation for belles-lettres.

As far as is known, no club has tried to hire Mason or others like him; perhaps it is cheaper for the clubs in the long run, by holding up rich prizes that only very few can win each year, to divert from other work a sizable number of the nation's writers and editors who compete for club selection.

BOOKS FROM THE MOVIES   How frequently publishers have issued books originally written for or sponsored by movie companies is a trade and often a personal secret. The conversion of original movie stories or shooting scripts into novels is a phase of this activity. One book written from such a script is William Saroyan's *The Human Comedy*, which Saroyan wanted to publish in script form. His publishers rejected this idea and hired a ghost writer experienced in making such conversions for magazines to make the script into a novel. Saroyan rejected her draft. He then wrote the novel himself, and it became a Book-of-the-Month Club selection and a best seller.

But Harcourt, Brace, Saroyan's publisher, probably would

have wanted to issue any novel by this author even without movie incentives. The same is true of anything by Carl Sandburg, another Harcourt, Brace writer and author of the MGM-subsidized *Remembrance Rock*. More to the point is *Sorry, Wrong Number*, a novel by Allan Ullman from the script by Lucille Fletcher, published in 1948 by Random House in time for movie tie-in sales. *Miracle on 34th Street*, a novel written by Valentine Davies from his original movie story, is another example. Harcourt, Brace published this in time to profit from movie publicity. Big sales, however, failed to materialize, partly because the movie was released in June, a poor month for launching a book, but the Book-of-the-Month Club chose *Miracle on 34th Street* as a Christmas present for its members and gave away many thousands of copies.

This sort of publishing simply gives professional Hollywood writers, by their own work or that of ghosts, the chance to appear as novelists. More important for the whole literary and publishing scene are other practices by which the movies have turned potential or established novelists into writers essentially for Hollywood.

Until their 1948 business and political jitters, the big movie companies and their stars believed they had money and prestige to gain from books "famoused up" in advance by trade publishers. Thus, they were most aggressive in seeking publisher-promotion of movie-selected manuscripts. When they have regained their liberty to spend and to speak, they may be expected to press for this again.

The highly publicized six-figure payments once made by movie companies for a few novels each year were enough to induce many writers to turn their talents to such work. A more formal inducement was the novel contest. MGM's 1947 contest announcement said:

$250,000 will be awarded to the author, contingent upon sales. $150,000 minimum will be guaranteed to the author. $25,000 will be awarded to the winner which is a choice of the Book-of-the-Month Club or the Literary Guild. $25,000 will be awarded to the publishers of the prize winning novel.

The winner that year was *Raintree County*. Other movie companies, independently or jointly with trade houses, have offered prizes or fellowships to writers. Farrar, Straus; Reynal, Hitchcock (now part of Harcourt, Brace), and others have had agreements with movie companies for the payment of such awards. From one series of fellowships offered independently in the middle 1940's, Twentieth Century-Fox placed more than fifteen novels with trade publishers. Some of them have not yet been made into movies.

Other awards attracted more immediately useful movie material; but even with the most attractive financial bait, contests and fellowships are haphazard, and good properties slip through. To tighten up movie-publisher relationships, agreements such as those between MGM and Random House and MGM and Farrar, Straus (referred to in Chapter I) were made. By their terms scouts paid by publishers and movie companies hunt for manuscripts and authors with plans for manuscripts suitable for trade publication and movie production.

The following story from *Publishers' Weekly*, October 11, 1947, tells of other editorial activities by movie companies.

Random House, they say, was in receipt of a wire from Darryl Zanuck one day during the summer suggesting that the title for "For Fear of Little Men" be changed to "A Shamrock for Stephen." Over at Random there ensued much stir and bustle. No author had been mentioned in the wire, and nobody on the staff knew of any book called "For Fear of Little Men." Further communication revealed that Twentieth Century-Fox had bought the Guy and Constance Jones novel before the publishers had even received it. At the present moment, novel and movie alike are slated to emerge as "There Was a Little Man."

Enlightening, too, is the story of the 1947–48 Doubleday best seller *So Dear to My Heart*. This book was originally a juvenile, *Midnight and Jeremiah*, written by Sterling North and published in 1943 by the John C. Winston Co. Very few copies were sold, and Walt Disney Productions bought all the rights to it for a small price. When the movie was well along, Disney employed Albert E. Sindlinger's audience research organization. Sindlinger's tests showed there was much public interest in the basic story. As a result North undertook to write for Doubleday an adult novel on the theme. This turned out to be completely different from the unsuccessful juvenile and was published by Doubleday in November, 1947. *So Dear to My Heart* was the December, 1947, selection of the People's Book Club.

ART AND "DEMOCRACY"   Sterling North (with twenty-four papers, the nation's most widely syndicated book reviewer) says he has become "genuinely converted" to Sindlinger. He adds: "People who scoff at poll-taking . . . are scoffing at democracy. . . . It is a humbling but enlightening experience. . . . I can think of several opinionated American authors who might benefit by the experience." It is not known which opinionated authors North had in mind, but some have in fact been Sindlingerized—still another process by which trade publishers, as *Time* put it, are "willing to discard their taste and editorial judgment for the promise of a relatively sure thing."[19]

Sindlinger is a former Gallup executive who "thought he knew a little something about what the public wants." On leaving Gallup, in 1946, he set up his own organization to translate what he knew into Broadway hits and best-selling books. *Time* describes how he works:

At his New Entertainment Workshop on a farm in Hopewell, N.J., a staff boils down the author's manuscript to a one-hour

[19]*Time*, February 2, 1948 (Courtesy of *Time*. Copyright Time Inc., 1948).

reading which is then recorded. The records are played in various cities and towns to hand-picked groups who first munch refreshments, and then all sit down together to hear the boiled-down book read, and record their impressions throughout (from "superior" to "bad") on an electronic gadget called Teldox. When it's all over, a composite graph indicates the weak spots in the story and the author is called in to make repairs. Whatever survives these sievings through the mass mind, Sindlinger says, is a story that's sure to sell.

Besides *So Dear to My Heart*, Sindlinger maintains that he has had a hand (how important or extensive his contributions have been is a subject of dispute between him and various publishers) in a number of other books, including *Sir Pagan*, a first novel by Henry J. Colyton, published by the Creative Age Press. He is also working on "mass writing by 'established writers,'" among them James Burnham, whose first "screen play" is being "developed by Mr. Burnham and the editorial staff of the Workshop with the help of what Sterling North calls 'the collective wisdom of the American people.'"[20]

THE PAYOFF   Though trade publishers have begun to accept manuscripts from reprinters, book clubs, movie companies, and market experts, they continue to get the bulk of their manuscripts in more familiar ways: from older authors already on their own or other publishers' lists, and from agents, "friends of the house," and scouts. The latter have become active "to a point near absurdity," as Ken McCormick puts it, particularly among college students, who also have been drawn to writing careers by many new prizes and literary fellowships.[21] A great number of manuscripts, most of them worthless, come in unsolicited—"over the transom," as the

[20]*Ibid.*

[21]On this theme James T. Farrell writes, in *The Fate of Writing in America*, p. 8: "A new occupation, that of literary scout, has been created. These scouts tour the literary sandlots of America, and with contract, check and fountain pen in hand, seek to sign up promising talent just as if they were

vernacular has it—while many more, especially in nonfiction, develop from editors' scanning of magazines and newspapers and their cultivation of professors, politicians, and others in the public eye. Many such experts or celebrities cannot write very well; consequently an increasing number of books are collaborative works between "names" with things to say and the "nameless" who say it for them. To some houses, notably Macmillan, Knopf, and Viking, many manuscripts come from abroad.

From this mass of writing—Doubleday alone receives more than 5,000 manuscripts a year—books to be published also are selected now much as they have been in the past. Prize-winning books and most others commissioned by the publisher naturally go on the list on delivery. Others are screened by readers inside or (especially for nonfiction) outside the office, then by the editorial staff and the sales manager. On controversial books the publisher himself may decide, though in large houses this is becoming less frequent.

Yet the newer outside elements are felt here, too. It is not unheard of for a trade house to postpone its decision on a manuscript, especially if it promises to be costly to manufacture, pending a major book club's expression of interest in it. Publisher-reprinter and publisher-movie relationships have been known to follow a similar pattern. Thus, these outside agencies, even when not promoting their own finds, work on the publisher's judgment; and if they did not, it would still be natural, given the easy money involved and the practice of entering it all as profit, for publishers and editors to be mindful, as they are, of these agencies' needs.

---

scouts for a major league baseball team. The need for new writers explains the growth of the institution known as Writers Conferences which are conducted by an increasing number of universities all over the country. (In most instances the teachers at these conferences try to give the amateur writer the rudiments of commercial writing.) It explains the reason for the existence of so many literary prizes and fellowships offered by publishers."

Yet the payoff from such agencies to an industry doing an annual business of $90,000,000–$100,000,000 does not seem commensurate with the power they exert. For 1946 the total royalty pool from hard-cover reprints (at royalty rates from 3 cents to 10 cents a copy) was about $2,300,000; from paper-bound, pocket-sized reprints (at 1 cent a copy on the first 150,000, and 1½ cents beyond that) about $1,250,000— making a sum of $3,550,000. The estimated 1948 figure for reprint royalties is about $3,625,000, all of the increase coming from the paper-bound books, sales of hard-cover reprints falling off that year. But these royalties, like those paid by book clubs, are split 50–50 by original publishers and authors, leaving $1,800,000 for the fortunate or far-sighted original publishers sharing in the 1948 pool.

This is only half the story; the other half concerns the clubs. For its 1946 selections (not counting dividends and bonuses) the Book-of-the-Month Club paid royalties (at 30 cents a copy for single selections and 20 cents a copy for dual selections) of almost $1,750,000; the Literary Guild's payments (at 15 cents on the first 500,000 copies and 18 cents thereafter) were almost as large, since the Guild sold more books. The royalties paid by all the other clubs must have swelled the 1946 total to about $4,000,000. The estimated figure for 1948 is $3,750,000, leaving $1,875,000 for publishers of originals sharing in club disbursements. Thus, from reprint and book club royalties the participating original publishers in 1948 divided an estimated $3,675,000.

Of the large sums once paid for books by movie companies, the publisher's share has varied from house to house and even within houses, from author to author, and from book to book. In the 1930's many publishers split movie money 50–50 with authors, just as they did reprint and club royalties; other publishers were satisfied with one third; still others with one fourth, a share still common from unagented authors and any others who can be induced to grant it. Yet some publishers have never claimed any part of movie money, and in recent years whether or not under pressure from authors' agents, others have adopted this policy.

To support their right to movie payments, publishers point to their risk in undertaking a book, their investment in it, and their creation of market value for it. During the wartime and postwar boom in movie buying their case was strengthened by the making of "escalator" contracts with movie companies by agents and authors.

A representative contract of this type may show that a company paid $50,000 for the movie rights to a book and an additional 40 cents a copy for each one sold beyond 50,000. Other clauses may have obliged the movie company to pay $25,000 more if the book should become a Literary Guild or Book-of-the-Month Club selection and $15,000 additional if the book were serialized in a national magazine. Most such contracts protected the movie company by stipulating a payment ceiling, in this instance perhaps $150,000.

Since such earnings seem to depend in part on publishers' selling ability, another type of contract between author and publisher has been developed to stimulate publishers' sales efforts. This is the Authors' League's "minimum contract," stipulating that the original publisher, under certain specific terms requiring the use of this money for advertising and promotion, may be allowed up to 15 percent of the total movie price for a book. Many agents and authors are opposed to the grant, and many publishers to the terms that hedge it in. The contract was written in 1947; by the end of 1948 only Random House had accepted it, though negotiations with other publishers were in progress.

Yearly payments for movie rights can be only roughly estimated; in 1948 they were probably the lowest in a decade or more during which, by any estimate, millions of dollars were spent each year. Movie companies, as has been said, also have agreed from time to time to bear part of publishers' sizable advertising and manufacturing costs for movie books. Tie-ins with poor movies have killed the sales of some original and many reprint titles, but successful movies have added to the publisher's take in direct sales revenue and royalties on reprints.

John O'Connor, president of Grosset & Dunlap and board chairman of Bantam Books, says that the estimated $3,675,000 in 1948 reprint and book club royalties paid to publishers of originals accounts for "two-thirds of publishers' total income from subsidiary rights," making the total about $5,512,500.[22] If this actually were all profit, it would be easier to understand why trade publishers, in shaping editorial and other policies, feel that only at their peril may they disregard subsidiary market opportunities.

Perhaps the greatest cost item in earning this subsidiary income, as well as that from best sellers in general, is the investment in the large number of candidates for such income that can never, in the nature of the markets, return much or any of it. The Book-of-the-Month Club and the Literary Guild together (royalties from most of the remaining clubs are small, even in the aggregate) sell or give away fewer than fifty titles a year.[23] Even when they were active in the market, the movie companies bought no more than that, and on most of the higher-priced ones, which often were identical with major book club choices, publishers received no cut. The annual combined total for hard-cover and paper-bound reprints is much higher than that for the clubs and the movies together, but reprinters' best sellers (which, at low prices, must sell very well in order to accumulate big royalties) are not very

---

[22]*Publishers' Weekly*, March 6, 1948.
[23]Actually, these and most other clubs sell *all* books; they run regular mail order businesses at retail prices, but this has no significance for publishers' subsidiary income.

numerous, and many of them duplicate club and movie selections. These are also likely to be the ones digested by *Omni-
book*, which has a monthly budget of $12,000 to spend on
four titles, or by the *Reader's Digest*, which may pay from
$1,000 to $10,000 for one book.

Thus, of the huge number of manuscripts examined by
trade publishers each year and of the four thousand or so that
they publish, perhaps no more than one hundred earn much
subsidiary income even when the movies are active buyers.
Scarcely one hundred more may, through the book stores,
compete for coveted places on the best seller lists, but here,
too, only those that remain at or close to the top for many
months sell in large quantities.[24]

[24]With very few exceptions, the most notable are the lists that appear in
Publishers' Weekly, best-seller lists are poor indicators of sales. Many of
them are based on misleading reports; virtually all of them rank books
only by their rate of sale for very short periods, usually one week; and
virtually none indicates the size of the gaps between the rates of sale of the
books ranked. These gaps can be enormous, as the following, from the
Sunday New York *Times Book Review*, January 16, 1949, suggests:
"The best-selling (in terms of bookstore sales) 1948 novel wasn't *The
Naked and the Dead* after all. 'Naked' was No. 2. Young Mr. Mailer had a
breath-taking head-start, and looked like the winner all summer and most of
the fall. But in mid-November along came Lloyd C. Douglas, and, whoosh,
the race was over. Mr. Douglas' *Big Fisherman* sold about 350,000 copies
in six weeks; 'Naked' about 125,000 in eight months."
The *Times* continues: "This suggests that Mr. Douglas is an old-timer,
with a ready-made audience. It suggests also, however, the uncomfortable
thought that those who hope to qualify as No. 1 popular novelist had better follow the formula.
"There have been few violations of the formula during the last fifteen
years. *Grapes of Wrath* (1939) was one, *Strange Fruit* (1944) another. On
the other hand, the list includes *Anthony Adverse* (1933, 1934), *Gone with
the Wind* (1936, 1937), *Forever Amber* (1945), *The King's General* (1946);
and *Green Light* (1935), *The Keys of the Kingdom* (1941), *The Song of
Bernadette* (1942), *The Robe* (1943), and *The Miracle of the Bells* (1947).
"The formula in short: (1) operate within a historical, costumed setting
or (2) develop a devotional theme. *The Big Fisherman* does both. *The
Naked and the Dead* does neither."
As for nonfiction, the New York *Herald Tribune*, October 24, 1948,
said: "For a generation or more, leading non-fiction best-sellers have been
pretty much of a piece: self-help, popularized religion, more self-help. The
only important variation came via certain topical titles during the war."

Of these top two hundred titles, then, fiction accounts, perhaps, for 150 each year, but even of this tiny number, at most one third, or some fifty titles, earn sums in six figures. Yet it is for such earnings that competition among trade publishers is most intense; even when they have stable incomes from backlists and diversified lines, the quest for spectacular long-shot payoffs may be said to dominate their thinking and the thinking of many of their authors as well.

MORE ON THE COMPETITIVE SITUATION   In this competition the big houses usually do best. Some authors, to be sure, are jealous of competing stars on large lists; others believe, sometimes with justice, that small houses can give them more favorable publication dates and better schedules for interviews, store and radio appearances, press conferences, and all the other occasions for book publicity. For these reasons popular authors sometimes ignore the blandishments of big houses and even shift from big to small ones. P.G. Wodehouse, for example, after many years at Doubleday, moved in 1948 to Didier Publishers. Yet the big houses are most widely known and receive more manuscripts than do the others. Agents prefer to deal with them, and agents supply about three fourths of the novels published each year and an even greater proportion of the best sellers. The bookstores look to the big houses for their sales leaders each season, thus making agents and authors still more favorably disposed toward them.

Thus, successful authors looking for bigger sales and mediocre ones hoping to get rich are most often drawn to the bigger houses because of their ramified markets and their good will in the stores. The big houses' advertising also catches bright writers on the make. Eight such houses had fourteen of the top twenty best sellers of 1947 (ten novels and ten nonfiction), and four others were published by Prentice-Hall; Longmans, Green; Lippincott; and Oxford University Press, none of them small houses even in the trade field.[25] Eight of the novels and seven of the nonfiction titles were also distributed by book clubs, either as selections or free books, some by more than one club. The average advertising outlay simply for launching each of these twenty books (an outlay often decided upon after a book club has made its selection) was $22,507; $40,000 to $60,000 was spent on a few of them.

Such sums cannot be promised or spent by most small houses; yet for each such outlay another large sum must also be risked on manufacturing a big first printing. Moreover, no house, large or small, can pick only winners, so that a number of best seller candidates, though backed at great cost, must be expected to fail. Small houses, particularly if they have no special lines and angels' money is running thin, cannot stand many such failures.

Most small houses, perhaps fortunately, are shut out altogether from another type of best seller-gamble—on topical nonfiction standouts like Byrnes' *Speaking Frankly*, Sherwood's *Roosevelt and Hopkins* (both Harper's), Hull's *Memoirs* (Macmillan), Churchill's *The Gathering Storm* and the subsequent volumes of his war memoirs (Houghton Mifflin), and *The Goebbels Diaries* and Eisenhower's *Crusade in Europe* (both Doubleday). Even such best seller candidates, because of the huge advances and other costly commitments often required in the hectic bidding for them, sometimes fail to pay off; yet when they succeed, they supply the big houses with more ammunition for the general contest. A few big houses also can offer authors and agents "package deals" for original publication and the exploitation of a "property" in many markets. Given the unstable and inadequate income of

[25]The best sellers are listed in *Publishers' Weekly*, January 24, 1948. The eight big houses are: Doubleday; Simon & Schuster; Viking; Houghton; Random House; Scribner's; Little, Brown; and Harper's.

most authors and their own rising living costs, such offers also must be very attractive.

THE PRESTIGE BOOK   With the strong tide against them running stronger, the future of the small houses may lie in flight from the mass markets to others in which serious literature may be made to yield a modest profit. But many small houses are interested neither in serious literature nor modest profits.[26] The others have before them the doleful history of many American publishers of the past who made the costly and usually abortive effort to develop enough writers and readers to support serious lists year after year.

Moreover, the large houses also compete for serious writers. Their concern with supplying what publishers themselves refer to as "pot boilers" for the book clubs, the reprinters, and the movies, does not mean their abandonment of serious literature. It takes the company of apparently serious books to lend the "pot boiler" the prestige that helps to make it pay. Besides, many commercial authors prefer to be on lists that carry serious writers, and the latter seem often enough to yield to the appeal of such lists. The extra money, of course, is important to them, but it is also pleasant for serious writers to think that big publishers may mean new and larger audiences for their art.

Mere contact with the new audiences, often won by meretricious advertising, which grows bolder as it cloys, has been known to change the art of serious writers; their success has

[26]Storer B. Lunt, president of W. W. Norton & Co., a small publisher of serious books, stated his view of the small publisher's position in a letter to the author, December 1, 1948: "Actually, I believe that the smaller publisher who is on his toes has very real advantages over the large publisher in the avoidance of habits, the weight of sustaining great overheads, and the entanglements implicit in over-organization. A bestseller on a large publisher's list sells no better than a bestseller on a smaller publisher's list, and the smaller publisher has, to my mind, as much or more opportunity for originality and individuality. However, it must be admitted that they don't all take advantage of this factor."

been known to move their publishers as well. Edwin Seaver, himself a novelist and the editor of *Cross Section,* an annual devoted to new writing by serious young authors, wrote of this in "The Age of the Jackpot," in the *Saturday Review of Literature,* February 15, 1947.

The real problem is not one of emergence but survival, not shall we have new writers, but can they grow up healthy and strong in our literary climate. . . . As long as a young author is working on his first stories or his first novel he is comparatively safe; he is still thinking of the word, of what he has to say and how he shall say it. If his first book fails to meet with popular approval the area of safety may be extended to his second. But once he is successful he is dragged into the vortex of the literary market place. In a milieu where nothing succeeds like success and dollars talk louder than words, with no authoritative criticism to guide him and no standards to serve as disciplines, he is a most unusual man who does not succumb to the lure of the big money. . . . There is no critical voice in the land with enough authority to stem the tide.

A case in point is Dr. A. J. Cronin. His 1948 hit, *Shannon's Way,* was advertised by his publisher, Little, Brown, with the headline, "No wonder it's a best-seller! It's his best*. . . ." The asterisk is part of the advertisement; it leads to a footnote in which William McFee, the New York *Sun's* reviewer, is quoted as saying: "The *best* novel Cronin has done in years." More germane is what McFee, in the issue of July 20, 1948, really said.

It is almost exactly seventeen years since we hailed a new novelist of remarkable power in the author of *Hatter's Castle.* G. W. Stonier in London discovered A. J. Cronin and we went along. We really believed a new planet had swum into our ken.

Everybody now knows Cronin for his phenomenal sales. Like those of C. S. Forester and other successful novelists, his worst books are his best sellers. The rich promise of *Hatter's Castle* has not been fulfilled. Dr. Cronin's fatal tendency to write below his full powers, his extraordinary addiction to adjectives, whether apt or not, grew on him. He began to write the same book over and over again. Why change, when the prescription was so successful and the patients cried for more and more of the same?

Shannon's Way is the best novel Cronin has done for years, the best since *The Citadel*. He may do a better one some day, but he is now in his fifties and is in a groove. He knows just what the patients want. As Somerset Maugham, another physician turned novelist, puts it, he prescribes "the mixture as before." *Shannon's Way* has all the Cronin characteristic strength and weakness, all the usual superabundance of adjectives, all the heavy leaning on dank, dark days with pouring rain to pile on the agony. It misses by a notch or two being the book this reviewer hopes Dr. Cronin will write. Like J. B. Priestley, he makes us admire his facility, and exasperates us because he is not better . . .

Of Carl Sandburg and *Remembrance Rock,* written simultaneously for MGM and Harcourt, Brace, Perry Miller said at the end of his front page review in the Sunday New York *Times Book Review,* October 10, 1948:

The book's orientation is not toward any philosophical thesis whatsoever, but toward a Hollywood production. With its judicious mixture of sex, battle, and sentiment, *Remembrance Rock* is a super-colossal script. . . . Whether wittingly or unwittingly, Carl Sandburg has written within the conventions of the panoramic film in technicolor. There is no more disheartening comment upon our era than to discover that at this point in his career the author of *Smoke and Steel* has lent himself to these maudlin devices.

These "cake-and-penny writers," as Seaver calls them, "want their compromise and their integrity too. But these, much more than the well-paid hacks, are the real despoilers of literature." Their defection makes it more difficult for small houses to develop serious lists and for serious houses to stay in business. Conversely, it allows the big houses to engross more of the trade-book field, and best sellerism and the quest for subsidiary markets to engross the energies of big houses and their authors.

CULTURAL RESPONSIBILITY   Despite these consequences and those of the more obvious kind of censorship imposed by religious, political, and outside business groups, the book industry remains at least as open to ideas of all sorts and to the work of young and mature artists who for a time may set themselves against the main trend as any other big American opinion forum, and more open than most. Newspapers, national magazines, moving pictures, radio and television, the pulpit, some school systems, and some colleges and universities, by becoming spokesmen for power groups or by yielding to their pressure, have surrendered much of their responsibility (if they had any) for free expression in America. Comparatively, in an age of increasing deference to the market and particularly in a period of constricting and sometimes panicky fear for national security, the book industry has kept itself remarkably liberal and free.

Yet in the present state of their business and of the public's opinion of it the publishers can scarcely be reminded of their responsibility too often. Even Congressmen, aware of book club advertising and the covers of most 25-cent reprints if nothing more, have become skeptical of the publishers' assertion that books are "the only permanent record of our culture, technology, and the highest intellectual and spiritual advances."[27] These Congressmen, in deciding on postal rates for books in 1947, questioned the publishers' right to postal leniency toward books; they may well have felt, in words used

[27]*Hearings* Before the Committee on Post Office and Civil Service, House of Representatives, Eightieth Congress, first session, March, April, 1947, Washington, D.C., Government Printing Office, 1947, p. 264. See also p. 276.

later by philosopher Irwin Edman, that the publisher has "exaggerated the cultural claims of works which one feels that he knew in his heart and mind were not contributions to the raising of the cultural level."[28]

Though the industry's record in nonfiction is better than in fiction, perhaps because writers of the best nonfiction are less beholden to the book market for their livelihood, even here ramparts have fallen. Keith Sward's *The Legend of Henry Ford*, a notable biography universally acclaimed now that it has been published, made the rounds of publishers, liberal and otherwise, for years. It was rejected only out of fear before Rinehart found the courage to issue and promote it and the Book Find Club the means to give it wide distribution. Paul Blanshard's book on the Roman Catholic Church, an expansion of his 1948 articles in the *Nation*, and Justin Gray's book on the American Legion, lesser works than Sward's, but scarcely on less important themes, were treated similarly for similar reasons, until they also found publishers—Blanshard's, the Beacon Press, a religious house, and Gray's, Boni & Gaer, a small trade house. Other important books on unpopular themes have been issued, in fiction and even in poetry, as well as in nonfiction, though some of them cannot be said to have been promoted with vigor and at least one of them, Robinson Jeffers' *The Double Axe and Other Poems*, was attacked (with the "cheerful consent" of the author, it must be said) for its political ideas by its own publisher on the very jacket of the book and in a "Publisher's Note" bound in it.[29] Only publishers and authors know how many other books have been edited with an eye to political and social conformity, and

[28]*Publishers' Weekly*, April 3, 1948. This issue has an extended report of a discussion among industry leaders on the publisher's "Cultural Responsibility."

[29]For an excellent review of this book and criticism of Random House's tactics by Ruth Lechlitner see the New York *Herald Tribune Weekly Book Review*, September 12, 1948.

how many others still, rating publication on literary or scholarly grounds, have never been published at all or on the advice of publishers have never even been written. These things, of course, have happened many times before; they are endemic to the book industry, as to all other communication industries. But in the past quarter century they have not happened so often as in the mid-1940's, when the publishers had the gravest responsibility to see that the standing of the book as a cultural vehicle, almost alone as a vehicle of free expression, was not driven down. The publishers' own awareness of their failure to meet this responsibility is shown by the American Book Publishers Council's announcement, February 5, 1948, "of the feeling among a growing number of members that the book publishing industry needs a public relations program." Yet nothing could attest more strongly than this announcement to the failure of these publishers even to understand how they have been remiss.

Many of the publishers and editors who make the decisions that narrow the intellectual and artistic scope and sap the vigor of the industry, or who suffer their legal departments to make them, or who acquiesce in the decisions of movie companies, book clubs, and reprinters on advertising policies, titles, and contents are nevertheless cultivated men, men of taste and conviction, who must often feel "debased and ashamed," as one serious writer said he felt on having his book selected by a book club and advertised sensationally. This writer said, perhaps naïvely, that while the club choice enriched him and for that he was grateful he would have preferred to have his book sold only to those of his friends to whose minds he felt he had been communicating. But of him the question may be asked: Why, then, submit the book to a publisher? Why not write it to friends? The answer, naturally, is that he is a writer of books for people to read. By this means he lives. And the publisher's answer is that he is a publisher of books for people to buy. They must give him a living.

Yet too much can be made by the publisher of his assertion that his censorship is the market's censorship—that he is the agent of the market. Being moral men, some publishers even now put on the market the best books they can find; they continue to publish works of intellectual and artistic distinction. And even now the hundreds of thousands who will buy the book club or the reprinters' choice will reject the publisher's own choice. Yet the common way out of this dilemma, to publish only more and more of what the market wants and to wash it down with public relations programs, may also be the common way to ruin. Perhaps that is the only way the publisher can afford to publish a little of what he likes himself, but as he concentrates on merchandise for the mass market, he may discover, if indeed he has not already discovered, that other work is more difficult to find and that the methods by which he raised the money for publishing the best literature available so lowered the intellectual and artistic vigor of writers that their best became undistinguishable from the best sellers.

3

BOOK MANUFACTURE AND
PUBLISHING COSTS

DURING THE THIRTIES it could truthfully be said (and if the 1947–48 decline in book sales continues it may easily become true again) that most American booksellers had to be carried financially by the publishers and most publishers by the book manufacturers.[1] In those days the profits of trade publishers depended more than they do now upon bookstore sales, and many stores were permitted to stay in business even when their debts were unpaid for long periods. This left the publishers chronically short of cash for their debts to the manufacturers, but the latter had reasons of their own for not demanding payment. Book manufacturers in the thirties, though burdened with high fixed plant charges, normally had work for only one shift and ran at about 60 percent of capacity; to get more work, most of them were willing recklessly to extend publishers' credit and to lengthen their payment terms.

Indeed, the bitterly competitive book manufacturers offered publishers many other inducements for their business or heeded excessive publisher demands. Offered freely or on demand were low, often cut-throat, prices, free sample covers

[1]Very few trade publishers have their own manufacturing plants. A book manufacturer usually composes, prints, binds, and jackets a book. He may also have a foundry for plate making, though this is unusual. Most trade books are produced by book manufacturers; the rest are composed and printed by one company and bound and jacketed by another. In either case the work normally is done under contract with the publisher, a new contract being made for each book. What is said henceforth about the manufacturer applies most frequently to the binder in those instances where a job is not wholly done by a manufacturer.

and salesman's dummies, and "so many colors, patterns, sizes, shapes, and qualities of material," as a report early in the period put it, that to furnish them "is now a heavy burden on the manufacturers and their suppliers."

More important, some manufacturers, nominally without charge, though the cost may have been charged as overhead, warehoused the publisher's plates, paper, printed sheets, and bound books, and gave him the privilege, again at little extra cost, of having books bound in as small quantities as the demand seemed to warrant. Since binding charges then, as now, were a large part of total manufacturing costs, publishers could, for example, print sheets for 4,000 copies, bind and receive only 1,500, ask the manufacturer to store the rest, and call for them to be bound in lots of 500. Only on delivery would the publisher be billed for binding, and then only for the lot delivered. This reduced his risk and spread his financial obligations.

Given the then normal state of publishers' payments, a manufacturer's offer of nominally free warehousing may have been his way simply to keep his hand on publishers' property, and his willingness to bind in small lots may have been a convenient hedge against investing too much of his own money in publishers' risky books. But these practices also earned work for the manufacturer's plant and thus helped to pay the fixed charges; they also helped to offset the cash advantage of richer over poorer publishers, the cost advantage of big over small editions, the marketing advantages of quick-moving best sellers over long-term, backlist titles.

Taken together, the terms under which books were manufactured before the Second World War probably put on a more equal footing than now the serious publisher with small lists and slow sellers and the big merchandising houses. Those terms made it easier than it is today for publishers to take risks on special works with limited markets, experimental books with unpredictable sales, and scholarly works with long-term, even if initially small, demand. They made it easier to keep standard works in print and scientific works up-to-date.

"THE TRADE WANTS UNITS, NOT LITERATURE" Thus, while other prewar circumstances may have forced trade publishers toward the star system and the best seller, there was nothing extraordinary in the manufacturing situation to prod them strongly in that direction. But war and early postwar conditions changed all this.

The wartime demand for almost every sort of book started a boom that ran from the spring of 1943 through 1946 and promptly brought into use all idle book manufacturing equipment. Soon many plants were employing two or three shifts, and others lagged only because of the shortage of new machinery and the scarcity of skilled workers. The longer the war lasted, the better the book business became, and manufacturers who a few years earlier had been seeking work almost on any terms became swamped with it and embarrassed by the increasing lateness of deliveries. The demand for huge quantities of school and college textbooks following the war was a new challenge to the book manufacturing industry.

To meet unprecedented problems, many manufacturers took steps that added to the difficulty of publishing special and scholarly books. Much storage space in manufacturers' plants was soon converted to more remunerative uses. Next, publishers were obliged to bind entire printings, pay for them in full, and have them shipped to fill unprecedented orders or removed to their own warehouses or shipping depots. Partly because of government regulations and the levying of plate storage charges by some manufacturers, but mainly because the metal was needed for new production, publishers also were compelled to melt plates for many backlist titles and were discouraged from preserving plates of recent publications.

But these changes still left manufacturers far short of meeting the growing demand. To step up production further, many of them reviewed their customary production methods and, according to their findings, shifted the alignment and location of departments and machines. The next logical moves were the standardization as far as was practicable of book sizes and other design specifications, and eventually the reduction and in some instances the elimination of time and labor for making press and binding equipment ready for short runs. In some plants such runs were delayed until time for them could be snatched from bigger projects. In others they came to be accepted only at premium prices. In still others they were almost always rejected in favor of large editions, particularly those of the major book clubs and the big trade houses that were most likely to have book club choices and other best sellers. After the war some manufacturers gave priority to the huge orders from school and college textbook houses and from integrated firms with school and college departments.

Many manufacturers, of course, had had good relations with certain publishers for years, and in recognition of such relations and in anticipation of the eventual end of the sellers' market, were more or less lenient in applying the new terms. Yet, generally speaking, these were the terms under which book manufacturing had come to be conducted, and they were reflected in the changed attitude of some of the manufacturers themselves. One of the largest of them said in 1946: "I have no use for small publishers. Why should I take time for make-ups on small runs, when I can run 20,000's? The trade wants units not literature."

A SELLERS' MARKET IN BOOK PRODUCTION　　This attitude and the conditions that fostered it became less prevalent as the textbook demand leveled off and trade business continued to recede from its 1946 peak. It continues to be reflected, however, not only in some manufacturers' choice of work, but also in the prices charged for work accepted. Most publishers object to these prices, because, their market being recruited largely from those segments of the population most severely hit by the inflation, they cannot pass them on; but they also object because of the manufacturers' apparent pricing formula. This runs: "materials plus labor plus 100 per cent"; from which it may be seen, as one publisher said early in 1948, "that the larger the costs, the larger the [manufacturers'] profits."[2]

But even if the manufacturers were to alter their formula and cut their profits, publishers' manufacturing bills would remain much higher than before the war. This is due to the sharp rise since 1942, and particularly since 1946, in the cost of manufacturers' equipment, materials, and labor. Prices of some printing and binding machinery have more than doubled since 1942; one type of press which that year cost $23,000, in 1948 cost $60,000. The prices of metals used in composition and plate making, and of boards, cloths, glues, and other materials used in binding, have risen steadily. Wages also have soared. According to Herbert Shrifte of the H. Wolff Book Manufacturing Co., as of March, 1948, wages of compositors were 81 percent above prewar levels; of journeyman binders, 70 percent; and of unskilled workers, 110 percent.

Another key element in manufacturing costs is the price of paper, which practically all publishers supply to the book manufacturers. Despite steadily increasing production during the war, paper of all types was short. By 1948 deliveries had about caught up with demand, but prices continued to rise. Since book paper was most acutely short and may still be difficult for small users to get promptly, prices on it have risen more than on other types of paper and remain high.

[2]*Publishers' Weekly*, February 21, 1948.

During and shortly after the war some big paper users, fearing a long-term world shortage of wood pulp which would endanger paper supplies, either bought up mills that once manufactured varied lines for the free market or contracted for a number of years' full output of large independent producers. This cut the production of book paper. It was cut further when big users also offered prices on the free market that made it "more profitable for independent mills to fill large magazine orders than to fill book paper requirements."[3]

A few of the "captive" mills have since returned to general lines, including book paper, and the older free mills, with the demand off for other types, have also restored or increased book paper output. Prices, however, largely because of paper manufacturers' own rising costs, have not responded to the improvement in supply. Late in 1948 book publishers' paper costs were about 50 percent above 1940 levels; some put the increase as high as 100 percent.

THE COST PICTURE   Trade publishers who have tried to estimate over-all increases in manufacturing costs differ on the exact figure, but agree that these costs have become onerous, that they are likely to remain so for some time, and that they already have had dire editorial consequences which will become disastrous if costs go higher—indeed, if they do not soon come down.

This position has had value for some publishers in their negotiations with authors and agents as well as with manufacturers. It was buttressed in 1947 by a series of statements in the *Saturday Review of Literature*, the *Atlantic*, and other journals by industry spokesmen such as Bennett Cerf, Cass Canfield, and the late Alfred R. McIntyre. These maintained, in Canfield's words, that "manufacturing costs . . . have

[3]*Publishers' Weekly*, January 3, 1948.

nearly doubled in the past few years."⁴ George P. Brett, Jr., president of the Macmillan Co., said in March, 1948: "While it is possible to take a choice of estimates of over-all cost increases, all costs have increased since 1940, between 60 and 70 percent."⁵ His company, of course, has many economies of large-scale operation.

Much more detailed than these estimates is the 1946–47 *Statistical Report* of the American Book Publishers Council, which summarized item by item the increases in manufacturing costs between January, 1942, and April, 1947.⁶ Perhaps most striking in this summary were the differences between the greatest and the smallest increases reported for each item. The greatest increase of all was for linotype composition— 138 percent (the smallest reported for this item was 33 percent). The smallest increase reported was for coated paper— 5 percent (the greatest for this item was 87 percent). Based on data from twenty-seven publishing houses, most of them issuing original trade books, this report showed *average* increases ranging from 37 percent for offset paper to 77 percent for linotype composition.

Raymond C. Harwood, general manager of Harper's and chairman of the American Book Publishers Council's Statistical Committee, has compared the council's 1946–47 *Statistical Report* and Cheney's *Survey* of 1930–31. He shows that while in Cheney's time *manufacturing* took an average of 35.7 cents of the publisher's revenue dollar, by April, 1947, when to be sure there were appreciably higher absolute outlays, it took an average (based on thirteen firms reporting to the council) of 38.8 cents. This is an increase over Cheney's figure of only 3.1 cents on the dollar, or 9.2 percent.

⁴See *Saturday Review of Literature*, July 12, and August 30, 1947; *Atlantic*, October, 1947.
⁵*Publishers' Weekly*, March 13, 1948.
⁶The full table appears in Appendix B.

The council later surveyed manufacturing costs for the
period April, 1947, to April, 1948, and found additional average increases for most items of almost 10 percent, though some
firms reported no increases at all. Some publishers reporting in
1947–48 had not reported in 1946–47, and vice versa. To
make the cost averages in the two reports comparable, the
council's 1947–48 statement used data only from houses reporting both years. The 1946–47 averages used in the second
report are higher than those in the first, so it is probably fair
to assume that these are all rather high-cost houses; yet even
among these, the percentage increases in the highest-cost
groups over Cheney's averages, as shown in the table below,
are not huge.

The following table shows manufacturing and other publishing costs in percentage of the publisher's revenue dollar
and as averages of groups of highest and lowest percentages
reported to the American Book Publishers Council for each
item, compared with Cheney's industry-wide averages for
1930–31.

	A.B.P.C., 1947–48[a]		A.B.P.C., 1946–47[a]		Cheney, 1930–31
	LOW	HIGH	LOW	HIGH	
Manufacturing	40.7	49.9	40.6	47.7	35.7
Royalty	13.9	18.6	14.3	18.3	17.3
Editorial	3.5	5.8	3.3	4.7	2.1
Selling	14.8	22.4	14.0	20.0	18.8
Shipping	2.3	4.8	2.3	4.6	1.9
Other overhead	12.4	19.9	12.3	18.1	18.3

[a]The same publishers reported each year.

Manufacturing costs have been made most of since they
have risen most, though not as much over 1930 costs as over
those for 1941 or 1942. Still they do not tell the whole story.
With the growth of paper work, office workers in publishing houses have grown in number, and generally their slim
prewar salaries have been raised. So have the salaries and
bonuses of many publishing executives. Expenditures for rent,

utilities, travel, and entertainment likewise reflect the general rise in the cost of doing business. Perhaps the smallest increases, generally speaking, have been in authors' royalties; while publishers' sales and prices have gone up, royalty terms have fallen appreciably.[7]

THREE SOLUTIONS FOR HIGH COSTS

Editorial.—Besides passing some of the new costs on to their authors, particularly their newer, younger authors, many publishers have attacked the cost problem on three levels: editorial, price, and production. Editorially, the attack has been easiest to manage, for here the publishers had only to move further in the direction—toward more best sellers, book club choices, reprint candidates, and books aimed at movie and digest markets—in which they were already moving rapidly for other reasons.

If the easy money from such books had not been sufficient to attract publishers to them, the risk in publishing less popular works would have gone far toward settling the issue. Until 1942 or 1943, on most books with sales of 2,500 copies, and comparatively few sold that many, trade publishers could break even. Virtually all publishers were willing to take chances on serious titles, even when expecting such low sales. Today the break-even point for most trade books is between six thousand and ten thousand copies. If more serious books could be expected to achieve such sales and achieve them within a few months, more trade publishers even now would

[7] The normal royalty scale for most trade books has long been 10 percent of the retail price on the first 2,500, 12½ percent on the next 2,500, and 15 percent thereafter. Many successful writers, once they were established, received 15 percent flat on all books. Some authors in the past few years have been cut to 6 percent to start, and the jumps have been widened. Some houses now never go to 15 percent of the retail price; other houses now apply the old percentages to the wholesale price, which is usually 35 to 40 percent below the retail figure. For some authors rising sales have kept their actual royalties from falling this much.

be interested in them. As it is, some publishers who have such books under contract hope they will never be submitted. Others have removed some serious titles from their future lists. Many refuse to make new contracts for unpromising sellers even at low royalty rates.

Publishers, of course, will continue to list many books whose sales will never reach six thousand copies, but they are making every effort to avoid most such books and their authors. The accumulation of remainders in 1948 and early 1949 made publishers more wary than ever of such books. Costs being what they are, especially for small editions, most publishers would rather always aim at sales of 10,000 copies or more, and hope that a few club selections each year will more than cancel the losses on those that fail to reach that figure.

As for older serious and standard titles: what wartime plate destruction started the new cost conditions accelerated. It is true that some titles for which old plates were still available have been reissued at higher prices than the earlier editions, thus to become profitable backlist items. This practice, however, has not measurably improved the out-of-print situation, which was so serious in 1948 that Carl Milam, then executive secretary of the American Library Association, said public libraries often could not spend more than two thirds of their appropriations for replacements, because so many standard books were unavailable. Milam's remarks applied in part to juveniles, where the out-of-print situation was worst. But he was speaking of adult books too.

Prices.—Besides forcing many trade publishers to cut their backlists and to limit the number of new titles of backlist caliber, rising costs have forced them to charge more for the books they do publish. For some time, price increases were only nominal, and even at their peak they have remained well below those of most other commodities and below the

increases in publishers' costs. At the end of 1947 *Publishers'
Weekly* estimated that since 1938, the average price of trade
books had gone up only 25 percent, practically all of it since
1945. Since then perhaps another 10 percent is all that publishers have dared pass along to consumers.

The past few years, to be sure, have seen the unprecedented
$5.00 (one-volume) novel and others at the once rare price of
$3.50. Moreover, the first $5.00 novel led the best seller lists
for many months, even after later printings had been priced at
$5.75. Other $5.00 and even $6.00 novels have also sold well.
In nonfiction, the sales of popular books at prices ranging
from $6.50 to $10.00 have also been remarkable. Most publishers, however, have refused to take the success of these
books as a cue for more drastic price rises. For each high-
priced success they can point to many high-priced failures.
Most of these probably would have failed at any price, but
others, many publishers believe, suffered from buyers' price
resistance.

Prices for books probably will not soon go above their
1948–49 peak. Most publishers have a healthy fear of competition from other entertainment industries and an awareness of the extraordinary inflationary pressure on their particular group of consumers. Hence, few of them look to price
increases as the solution for rising costs and declining profits.

New production policies.—Though few publishers are optimistic about the effect on costs of new book production
policies, some of them have been experimenting on this third
line of attack. Savings have been sought chiefly in book design and in the scheduling of book manufacture.

Some of the experiments in design are in fact efforts to return, under supposedly normal conditions, to innovations first
tried during the war. Thus, publishers and, more frequently,
book clubs and reprinters are using lower grades of paper

than they woul have used earlier in the same books. They are also skimping on margins and, less frequently, on the size and clarity of type. They are publishing more short books and fewer illustrated ones and are using fewer color plates in books with pictures, particularly juveniles. They are substituting paper for cloth in binding, ink for gold in lettering. They are using less elaborate, less colorful jackets.

These changes have enabled publishers to shave costs somewhat and retard price increases. Changes in the scheduling of production, some of which can also be traced to wartime precedents, have had similar results. During the war, by taking great pains and ignoring long delays, publishers could get book paper and other materials in all sizes, colors, and shapes. Most publishers, however, limited their books to a few sizes and to certain standard specifications within each size. This made it easier for manufacturers to schedule series of books with identical specifications and thus sharply reduce the time-consuming adjustments of composing, printing, and binding machines. Changeovers from book to book, even among the smaller editions of different publishers, could often be made simply by changing the plates. The manufacturers' wartime preference for big runs reduced even plate changes to a minimum and helped them get out the maximum number of units.

Yet, to sell, books must catch the public eye; ordinarily a publisher wants each book to appear a little different from all others, even from those on his own list. Thus, with the return to peace many publishers resumed their prewar competition in design. As the production bottleneck only worsened, however, the many book styles and hence the frequent time-consuming make-readies irked manufacturers more than ever and caused publishers themselves many delays and additional expense. A return to standardization was indicated.

Publishers started, of course, on their own lists. Then, in a move without precedent in the industry, a number of smaller publishers agreed to design their books in consultation with each other so that those of the whole group could be printed and bound in large blocs with a minimum of machine adjustments. The time required for production executives to consult on each bloc, however, to make it up, and to win the cooperation of the manufacturer in each case, soon proved too great. Moreover, some participating publishers were disappointed in the savings. Some manufacturers also opposed the arrangement.

Though the group quickly fell apart, an indication that its work may nevertheless have lasting results was given, early in 1948, when the Colonial Press, one of the largest book manufacturers, announced a new type of manufacturing contract called the "A plan." Colonial offered to charge about 10 percent less than its normal quotations for jobs with certain standard specifications. The first set applied to books printed on sheets 44″ by 66″. Since then specifications have been issued for sheets of other standard sizes.

Sixteen per cent of our December business was on the A plan [said Harold Smith, president and sales manager of Colonial, early in 1949]. Publishers like it, and we're going to continue it. We're going to have to crack down on deviations from it, though. After all, it's a plan for economies through standardization. If we make one exception here, and another exception there, as publishers are urging us to do, by and by we'll be back where we started, with no two books alike.[8]

Though business has continued to be exceptionally good for book manufacturers, the expansion of older plants since the end of the war and the opening of a few new plants (of which the Doubleday factory at Hanover, Pennsylvania, is the largest) has cut appreciably into their backlog of work. The falling off of trade book sales since 1946 has also lessened

[8]*Publishers' Weekly*, February 5, 1949. This issue contains a detailed article on the "A plan" by Daniel Melcher.

the pressure on the manufacturing industry. These conditions and the general uncertainty of the business future in a highly inflationary period have caused many manufacturers to wonder if their sellers' market is passing. Colonial's new contract surely was a sign of the return to competitive selling by manufacturers. Even more significant was the offer made to trade publishers in June, 1948, by the American Book-Stratford Press, Inc., also one of the largest book manufacturers.

This offer proposed an attack on high costs not through improved production methods but through radical changes in the whole relationship of publishers and manufacturers. "All that is asked of the publisher," said Sidney Satenstein, president of American Book, in a circular describing the plan, "is the support that he can give by placing at least 80 percent of his volume of manufacturing in one firm, thereby giving such a firm the basis for the volume required to bring down costs." A publisher agreeing to this, "buys his manufacturing at a fixed percentage of the retail price" of each book, the percentage being "determined by evaluation of the publisher's policy, lists and sales records."

The plan, if it works, will cut costs appreciably, especially of small editions, on which present costs are most onerous. There is widespread endorsement of it on this account. In operation, however, it seems to require publishers to disclose to this manufacturer extremely detailed and often heretofore confidential information. It also requires them, in many instances, to terminate long-standing good relations with other manufacturers in order to give this one the required volume. For these reasons there has been much reluctance to sign up, especially among publishers not already big customers of American Book.

AN IMPENDING TECHNOLOGICAL REVOLUTION   In making his proposal Satenstein said that "the book manufacturer can no

longer consider himself an isolated segment of the industry";
it may be that his plan and Colonial's are signs that the different
parts of the industry are learning to work together. Encouraging also is the willingness of a few manufacturers to
experiment with radically new book production techniques.
On this score Milton Glick, in charge of production at Viking, said early in 1948:

Our real quarrel is not with our book manufacturers but with
their old-line equipment suppliers, though we do deplore such
apathy on the part of the majority of book manufacturers as permits them to stand in line awaiting very expensive old-style
equipment instead of pursuing . . . others who have exciting developments in the works, some of which are adaptable to our
problems.[9]

One cause of this apathy has been the manufacturers' fear
that the "exciting developments" may suddenly make their
heavily capitalized plants obsolete. Moreover, their time and
present equipment have for years been so fully occupied that
they are reluctant to deviate from tested production methods.
Nevertheless, some manufacturers have experimented along
new lines, and a few optimistic publishers look to these experiments for relief from mounting costs.

This optimism may be premature, but it is not altogether
unfounded. Experiments have shown, for example, that books
can be composed on a variety of new machines similar to the
ordinary typewriter and much less costly than linotype or
monotype equipment. If perfected, these new machines
would greatly reduce plate cost. Since books composed on
them would be printed by photo-offset and since ordinary
book paper cannot be used in some offset work, some publishers believe that this method of composition would scramble the paper situation and that the additional cost of offset

[9]*Publishers' Weekly*, March 13, 1948.

paper would cancel much of the saving on composition and plates. Also, some offset paper is not well adapted to folding and binding machines now in use. The proponents of the new method, however, argue that if it were perfected and widely used, offset paper better adapted to book manufacture would be produced.

These new machines may revolutionize book composition. Even if they do not, impending changes in letter press work itself may assure lower costs. Perhaps the most important experiments here have been in plate making, where lighter plastics, rubber, and magnesium have been used commercially in place of the traditional lead and copper. Skeptics point to the loss of clarity in the impressions from some of the new plates, the unevenness of the ink spread, and other difficulties. Proponents say these difficulties are easily overcome. In particular rubber plates (which Scribner's used at their North River press as early as 1942) are said to outlast metal plates, require less ink for the same amount of work, and save make-ready time. These advantages, however, have yet to be demonstrated conclusively.

Stahley Thompson, of Rinehart & Co., formerly with the Armed Services Editions, said early in 1948: "It was because of rubber plates that it was discovered that it is no longer necessary to have a press-run of 50,000 to successfully use a rotary press. You can successfully print with a rotary press down to about 15,000."[10] Thompson himself was responsible for such runs on Armed Services Editions paper-bound books, and he spoke with special reference to the 25-cent field. Most publishers in this field say that they cannot print in such small runs without raising their prices appreciably. *Publishers' Weekly*, September 11, 1948, reported that the Export Publishing Enterprises, Ltd., of Toronto, "will print first runs of 20,000 copies each" of 25-cent books in "fiction, detective,

[10]*Publishers' Weekly*, February 7, 1948, see also issue of August 2, 1947.

westerns, and self-help," but did not say how long such books will be.

In binding, perhaps the most important experiments have been with adhesives for attaching the case (the stiff covers and back) to the signatures (folded, cut, and gathered pages). Adhesives now generally used need at least four hours to dry; new ones dry almost instantaneously, but are brittle and require new and costly production equipment. The new adhesives would make binding a quick and continuous operation. Perhaps more money is now being spent on efforts to make them practical than on any other innovations in book manufacture.

BIG-EDITION ECONOMIES   *Publishers' Weekly* said in an editorial, February 7, 1948: "No one expects immediate changes in cost as a result of the new accumulation of discoveries." Less spectacular changes already in commercial use, however, have brought important savings, especially on long runs.

One of these changes is the adaptation of the Goss press to book work. This press is fed paper from a roll instead of a stack of flat sheets. Like other rotaries, it reduces paper cost by saving the expense of sheeting. It also cuts make-ready time and permits continuous, rapid printing. The Goss press delivers cut and folded sheets ready for gathering and thus eliminates a complicated step in the preparation of a book for binding.

The double folder and cutter has brought big savings on work not done on Goss presses. This machine can handle two books at once and thus halve folding and cutting time. The fully automatic sewing machine has also cut binding time on sewn books, while "perfect binding," in which the individual pages are glued directly to the spine, as in telephone books, has eliminated sewing altogether. "Perfect binding" is strong and inexpensive, but books so bound do not hold their shape as well as sewn ones. This makes the process unsatisfactory for expensive editions. Another time-saver is the automatic jacketer, which has eliminated a slow hand operation.

These and other new machines of proven merit are to be found only in a few big manufacturing plants. The others have lagged in their modernization as a matter of policy or because of the inability or reluctance of machinery firms to turn out new equipment. Virtually all the new devices have been installed in the new Doubleday plant at Hanover, Pennsylvania. Doubleday's huge Country Life Press, at Garden City, will continue to produce most of Doubleday's regular line of trade books and reprints; the new plant, significantly, will produce almost exclusively for Doubleday's book clubs. Its rotary presses will not be used for any books with first printings of less than 50,000 copies, though reprintings in smaller runs will be made.

THE FUTURE OF THE SMALL EDITION   Though a revolution in book manufacturing processes is clearly in progress, most regular trade publishers expect to escape from the present crisis in manufacturing costs—if they escape at all—not by changing their manufacturing techniques, but by altering their editorial policies. If costs must come down and if they can be brought down most on large editions, obviously the business-like thing to do is to publish books of immediate and widespread popularity, especially for book clubs, movies, and reprinters. In the traditional bookshop and department store markets, sales are highly unpredictable, so that even on best sellers there, print orders are likely to remain small and frequent. The big book club market, on the other hand, is most appealing: the big clubs can guarantee to sell each of their selections in the hundreds of thousands and frequently to stimulate the sales of the bookstore editions as well.

4

THE BOOK MARKETS

Speaking at the 48th Annual Convention of the American Booksellers Association, May, 1948, Robert B. Campbell, the association's newly elected president, said:

Perhaps the discussions at these meetings will result in conditions that will make the book business much more lucrative. I am not sure I want that to happen. If it is easy to make a lot of money in the book business, too many ordinary people will get in the business and spoil its fun for the bunch of—shall we say—characters who now operate it. These conventions, and life in the book business generally, would not be nearly as much fun if the majority were all shrewd, scheming business men and women instead of the truly remarkable group of eccentrics here assembled.[1]

If this pronouncement was a joke—a charitable view of it—surely at a convention where one of the subjects for discussion was "Book Sales in a Tight Market," it was an ill-timed one. It is not difficult to imagine how it was received by many publishers and sales managers and some leading booksellers who, while recognizing the strategic place still held by the bookstores in the distribution of serious literature, have long been painfully aware of the eccentric nature of many of those upon whom the defense of that place rests.

Campbell's remarks, presumably acceptable to the majority of booksellers who had named him their head, are alien neither in tone nor implication to the historical literature of his segment of the industry. Much of this literature is marked by a spirit of friendly intimacy with bookshops and their pro-

[1] *Publishers' Weekly*, June 5, 1948.

prietors and a warm regard for the idiosyncrasies of both. On the whole, it is not very informative about general book business conditions or about the changing stucture of the industry, but it does convey the booksellers' gradual loss of stature from the time in the nineteenth century when they were the kingpins of the whole book trade.

Many nineteenth-century booksellers seem to have been at once publishers, printers, wholesalers, and retailers; specialists in these branches of the industry probably did not seriously challenge their position until well past 1860. Thereafter, as the volume of American writing grew, more and more publishing houses were started, and independent printers and binders arose to handle their work. Before long, new types of booksellers appeared to perform the remaining functions of wholesaling and retailing.

Most of the old-line booksellers and many of the newer ones once carried large stocks of professional and business titles. Often, indeed, they sold general literature simply to eke out their incomes from printing and publishing and from the sale to individuals, libraries, and schools, of law and medical books, school textbooks, almanacs, directories, encyclopedias, and other reference works. But just as the older booksellers gradually lost some of their varied functions, so most of the newer ones eventually restricted their trade to general literature or to what are now called "trade" books. In the past thirty years specialization has been carried even further, so that now it is the rare American bookshop whose stock is representative of the whole range even of trade publishing.

Thirty to forty years ago, according to George P. Brett, Jr., president of the Macmillan Company, many American bookstores shelved at least one copy of every new Macmillan title; none does this today, even for the trade books alone. Other publishers probably can say much the same thing. For this the publishers themselves are partly responsible. The striking growth in the size of trade lists in the past thirty years has made it very risky for any but the largest stores to attempt to stock all titles. This risk has grown as best sellerism, with emphasis upon the advertising and promotion of only a small fraction of the titles issued, has become more marked. The risk has become greater still in more recent years, when best sellerism has been accentuated by the great increase in the value of subsidiary rights. Since publishers have fashioned their lists to attract book clubs, reprinters, and movie companies, bookstores have had to adapt their buying to this trend. They have also been discouraged from stocking more serious books ever since their loss, during the depression, of library and school business. Wholesalers and in a few instances publishers themselves captured this business by offering higher discounts than stores could afford to grant.

Yet it has been estimated (and figures being what they are, these are only informed guesses) that American bookstores have never sold more than one original adult trade book a year for every four adults (fifteen or older) in the population, and in 1948, despite a record national income, they did not even do as well as that. If the fifty best sellers in any year are omitted from the estimate, the ratio is much smaller still. Whatever the publishers' responsibility for this poor showing, the persistent bookseller attitude which makes a virtue of apathy toward improving it can scarcely be encouraging to those who must look to the stores to counterbalance the growing pressure on publishers' lists of club, reprint, and movie needs.

BOOKSELLER VERSUS PUBLISHER   Booksellers' nominal lack of interest in business matters or, in many instances, their lack of time or staff to deal adequately with them has not inhibited them from complaining bitterly about certain practices of the publishers and has not saved them from incurring complaints from the publishers. In the past few years, to be sure, these parties have found some new areas of agreement, notably in the handling of returns of dead stock and the granting of rebates for original books still on booksellers' shelves when cheap reprints of the same titles are issued. If the American Book Publishers Council's Ohio Plan, by which the publishers are re-evaluating their approaches to the booksellers and the booksellers' approaches to the ultimate buyer, is successful, other problems will be clarified, if not solved.[2] Yet almost everyone in the book industry agrees that there are still far too many areas of controversy between booksellers and publishers.

Many booksellers charge that publishers' payment terms are too short and their trade discounts too small, particularly on special orders for slow-moving staple titles. They charge publishers with being dilatory in filling reorders, with reneging on advertising promises, with shifting publication dates to satisfy book clubs and movie companies after advertising build-ups for earlier dates. They charge them with laxity in protecting publication dates, resulting in pet accounts that sometimes get the jump on more ethical stores in putting featured books on sale. They charge them with remaindering parts of editions while continuing to sell the same books to regular bookstores at original prices. Most booksellers, who find it difficult enough to select their stock from the great number of titles issued each year, complain of the additional burdens caused by publishers' failure to give advance notice of salesmen's visits and to see that salesmen, when they do appear, are fully acquainted with their lines. High-pressure selling, an evil in itself, heightens booksellers' antagonism to publishers on all other counts.

Publishers, in turn, often accuse booksellers of carelessness in ordering and tardiness in paying. They charge many book-

[2] See below, p. 103.

sellers with giving poor service and thus not earning the discounts they get. Booksellers are said to act as order takers when expected to push certain titles; to pay scant attention to backlist items; to fail to develop mailing lists or other special markets for special-interest books.

Most of these irritating charges and countercharges are probably unavoidable in the day-to-day business relations of mutually dependent firms usually undercapitalized and short of cash. As long as capital and cash shortages persist—which will probably be as long as there are trade publishers and booksellers—many of these problems are likely to persist. Disputes over them may be said to have become part of the climate of the industry—often creating an atmosphere of recrimination in which other and often more serious problems must be considered.

These problems do not result from the relations of booksellers with trade publishers, but rather from the latter's occasional efforts to bypass the stores. Though inured to it, booksellers still are resentful over their loss of school and library business. They are most concerned, however, about publishers' efforts to reach individual customers through the mails. This is done by coupon advertising, mainly of self-help and inspirational books, direct-mail advertising of similar books and professional and business literature, and book club distribution of the cream of the publishers' lists virtually always below retail prices and sometimes as free dividends and bonuses.

Controversy has raged most bitterly between booksellers and trade publishers over the book clubs (which are discussed below), but the publisher's own selling through the mails has also caused much hard feeling. The publishers and their representatives, however, seem to have justified these practices. A statement in *Publishers' Weekly*, March 20, 1948, by Victor O. Schwab, long a partner in Schwab and Beatty, one of the

biggest book advertising agencies, summed up the publishers'
case. Schwab said (the italics are his):

Any industry, regardless of the type of product which it manufactures, which has large production capacity and which makes
salable *consumer* products MUST have retail outlets adequate—in
quantity, location, financial stability, and selling aggressiveness—
to distribute those products. If it does *not* have them, then one of
the inevitable results is that the more enterprising of the units *in*
that industry will reach out to make direct sales-contact with the
public—by mail order advertising, direct mail circularizing, or individual representatives.

It may be that the limitation of retail outlets in an industry is
partly the natural result of geography, of sparsely-settled areas in
a country as far-flung as the United States. Or there may be large
areas where—because of educational standards, climatic conditions, economic circumstances, transportation difficulties, or general public indifference—it is not commercially feasible for retail
outlets selling certain types of products to operate successfully.

However, whether the limitation of outlets is justified or unjus-
tified is not pertinent to the present discussion. The point to remember is that (whether or not the *general* demand for a product
is sufficient to support a greater number of retail outlets) enterprising companies will continually be interested in ways of reaching out for the business of *individuals* who want their products—
individuals who (because of the inconvenience, inadequacy, or
complete lack of retail outlets) cannot or will not obtain them
locally. Into this breach steps the ubiquitous U.S. postman—
delivering periodicals, sales literature, or catalogues containing
mail-order offerings; carrying orders back; returning with merchandise.

In the book business the breach between the size of production
and the number and marketing areas of retail outlets is an exceed-
ingly wide one. Therefore, considerable mail-order activity in the
field is natural and inevitable. The office map of the book publisher's sales manager can show just a few little clusters of "retail
outlet" dots here and there on the vast surface of the area of the
United States!

MODERN BOOK OUTLETS   In the United States today there are probably no more than fifty bookstores (independent bookshops, units of chains, and book sections of department stores) which stock from three thousand up to twenty-five thousand adult backlist titles and three thousand to five thousand new titles each year, including technical and professional books. Perhaps 200 additional stores stock two thousand to three thousand current titles and about 1,000 adult backlist items, among which hobby and self-help books are most numerous.

These 250 stores plus 150 or 200 smaller ones in large cities are all that most regular trade publishers' salesmen call upon. Salesmen for larger firms may visit seven hundred to eight hundred more stores making about 1,200 that display a sufficient variety of original trade titles to warrant being called trade book stores.

Salesmen for two or three of the very largest original trade publishers may, among them, call at least once a year on as many as 3,000 "outlets," but most of the additional ones do an appreciable part of their total business in commodities other than books and a large part of their book business in lower-priced reprints, juveniles and self-help titles. Their stocks of new adult books are likely to be limited to a few hundred of those most widely advertised.

Smaller publishers of original trade books reach these smaller stores and practically all "institutional" accounts—mainly public and school and college libraries that spend about $20 million a year on trade books—through hard-cover wholesalers. Of these the American News Company and Baker & Taylor, in New York City, and A. C. McClurg & Co., in Chicago, are by far the three largest. They and a few others operating regionally also supply thousands of additional customers for publishers who have a wide coverage of their own. McClurg, for example, has about eight thousand regular accounts,

two thirds of them libraries and schools. Baker & Taylor has
more than ten thousand, about half of them institutional. The
American News Company, the largest wholesaler and the
only one with regional warehouses—forty of them—services
about twenty-five thousand "outlets."

Though each of these wholesalers has a few big accounts
that buy from it exclusively or reorder from it, often in expectation of more prompt deliveries than publishers can make,
most of their customers are small and as distributors of serious
literature insignificant. Nevertheless, almost one third of trade
publishers' sales for bookstore distribution, and as much as one
half by some companies, are made to wholesalers. American
News stocks fifteen to seventeen thousand titles (including
many low-priced juveniles); Baker & Taylor, at least twenty-
five thousand. All these titles may be catalogued, but most are
not otherwise on display. To get them through wholesaler's
accounts individual buyers have to be well enough informed
to ask for them, and the accounts alert enough to order what
is not in stock.

About five thousand drug and variety chain stores and sixty
thousand magazine outlets also sell books, though some drug
and variety chains that carried them during the war have since
given their space to bigger earners. Few of these retailers regularly stock titles priced above 35 cents; the drug and variety
stores sell juveniles, self-help books, and paper-bound reprints, the magazine stands mainly such reprints and occasional paper-bound editions, normally at $1, of new trade
books of obvious national interest.

Most drug and variety chains buy directly from the publishers of cheap books; the magazine stands are serviced by
magazine specialists. The American News Company, unlike
the other two big hard-cover wholesalers, is also one of the
largest magazine distributors, and through its facilities in that
field it sells Avon, Dell, and Popular books. The other paper-

bound books are distributed by the Independent Magazine Wholesalers, a group now of about eight hundred regional marketers originally organized in 1893 to combat the American News Company. These Independent Wholesalers are supplied by thirteen big national distributors, of which Pocket Books is one. Pocket Books sells directly to the Independents. Bantam Books are sold to them by the Curtis Publishing Company, another of the thirteen and part owner of Bantam. Fawcett Publications, a big magazine house and a third of the national distributors, handles the New American Library's books.

Besides American News and the Independents, there are the so-called "galley operators," who supply magazines and paperbound books to dealers in rural and some suburban places not otherwise reached. Seven major galley operators service about twelve thousand outlets in all parts of the country. In 1947 they accounted for 8 to 9 percent of New American Library's total business.

THE BOOKSTORE MAP Magazine distributors aim at having one outlet for every one thousand adults in the population. They have not quite attained this for either magazines or paper-bound books, but the problem of getting intensive nationwide distribution of such merchandise may nevertheless be said to be solved.

Somewhat more limited is the goal of the large publishers of cheap hard-cover adult books, and juveniles; they want at least one outlet in every community of five thousand or more. They virtually achieved this during the war, when almost every town that could support a Woolworth, Kresge, or Walgreen store or a link in any of the numerous regional variety and drug chains was likely to have an adequate cheap-book outlet. Though many chains have since stopped selling books, the twenty-five thousand hard-cover book outlets claimed by the American News Company indicates that numerous small communities must still support places where cheap hard-cover books can be bought. Many such places also display top new fiction best sellers, nonfiction leaders like Dale Carnegie's *How to Stop Worrying and Start Living* or Eisenhower's *Crusade in Europe*, and higher-priced reprints of major book club and movie novels.

For more varied adult fare and for higher-priced juveniles, the distribution map is neither so satisfactory nor so clear. An energetic bookseller even in a small or a medium-size town which does not ordinarily rate a visit by any regular publisher's salesman, may with the co-operation of big wholesalers do an excellent job of getting serious books to local readers and others in surrounding counties. In larger cities an enterprising bookseller's range is wider still. Frederic G. Melcher, of *Publishers' Weekly*, recalls that

for five years I managed a bookstore in Indianapolis, and my customers were all over the 8 adjoining counties, none of which had a city big enough for a good bookstore (If *local* buying runs about $1.50 per capita a year, it takes a city of at least 20,000 to have a successful shop). The book buyers came to Indianapolis for books, as for many other types of merchandise. And these people received catalogs and circulars.[3]

The jobs done in more recent years by Allan McMahon of the Lehmann Book and Stationery Co., of Fort Wayne, Indiana, or Fred Wood, of the Open Book Shop in Bridgeport, Connecticut, also are impressive.

In many towns and cities, on the other hand, and even in metropolises such as New York, Chicago, Washington, or Los Angeles, where there are scores of bookstores and competition is often keen, some shops are so slipshod that their very appearance repels prospective customers, and others are so carelessly managed that they not only fail to hold customers

[3]Letter to the author, July 2, 1948.

drawn to them but also alienate many such customers from dealing in bookstores at all.

In 1947 the American Book Publishers Council queried on a number of subjects, including their direct-mail activity, the 3,041 bookstores visited at least once a year by salesmen for two of the largest trade publishers. Of the 1,112 stores that responded, 578, or 52 percent, stated that they "maintain mailing lists of their customers." These lists often have the names only of local people with special book interests. Some, however, reach out beyond city or town limits and give suburbanites and even rural dwellers urban bookstore service.

Yet this service can be no better than that in the stores themselves. In most of them, as has been said, buyers of current best sellers and a limited number of other titles—and surely they are the great majority of buyers—are well served; those seeking serious current literature not heavily in demand or most backlist titles are frequently poorly served. For this publishers and wholesalers are not entirely blameless. Even when a bookseller has the enterprise to try to fill special orders (at discounts well below the 40 percent he often gets for stocking best sellers), he usually has to wait from one to as many as five weeks for the books, depending upon the section of the country.

Nevertheless, many booksellers who do have the initiative to expand their business and the traffic to warrant expansion generally do not have the required capital or credit. The capital now invested in bookstores is not known, but if it is related to sales—as indeed it must be—it cannot be large. The gross annual sales of each of the 3,041 bookstores mentioned above are unavailable. Dun & Bradstreet, however, reported in 1947 that the average American bookshop—excluding department stores—did a gross annual business of about thirty thousand dollars. But even this modest figure is misleading, as the following breakdown of a representative group of 740 mem-

bers of the American Booksellers Association indicates. This
table includes book sections in many large department stores.

Size of Stores by Gross Annual Sales 1946	Percentage of Stores
Under $10,000	32.0
$10,000–$24,999	23.0
$25,000–$49,999	18.0
$50,000–$199,999	21.0
$200,000–$499,999	4.0
$500,000–$999,999	1.6
$1,000,000 and over	0.4
TOTAL (=100 PERCENT)	740

Since ABA dues are on a sliding scale, increasing with members' sales volume (unaudited by ABA), the number of small
stores in the table may be too large. Also, some big department stores and chains are not members of the ABA; this reflects adversely on the number of big stores in the table. Yet
most bookstores not ABA members are very small. Were they
included, the most numerous group, doing less than a ten-
thousand-dollar business a year, would be very much bigger.

Clearly, even if there were in the United States many more
bookstores like most of those now in business, there still
would not be good bookstore service.

WHERE NEW BOOKS ARE SOLD   The American Book Publishers Council's 1946–47 *Statistical Report,* based upon the
experience of twenty regular trade publishers, listed the thirty-
two best American book-buying cities and the proportion
of national sales (in copies) made in each. This list, however, had serious faults. All sales made by wholesalers to outlets
in these and other cities were excluded from the total. Also,
publishers' sales to "a few large retail organizations throughout the country that purchase large quantities of books for
eventual sale through branches in many other cities than the

one serving as headquarters for the purchasing operation" were credited to the headquarters cities.[4] Obviously the council's list is awry and would best be ignored.

A more realistic list of best book cities, based on various 1947 data collected from a number of sales managers, was made by the vice-president in charge of sales of one of the leading publishing firms; this list, in which the cities are rated by him, is given here. Following the name of each city is the number of bookstores in it, from among the 3,041 stated above to be the only ones likely to be visited by any regular publisher's salesmen.

TWENTY LEADING BOOK CITIES (IN ESTIMATED ORDER OF IMPORTANCE) AND NUMBER OF BOOKSTORES IN EACH

City	Stores	City	Stores
1. New York	333	11. Cincinnati	24
2. Chicago	88	12. Minneapolis	19
3. Boston	46	13. Pittsburgh	20
4. Los Angeles	66	14. Indianapolis	11
5. Cleveland	22	15. St. Paul	11
6. Philadelphia	54	16. Baltimore	32
7. San Francisco	59	17. Buffalo	20
8. Detroit	23	18. Columbus	16
9. St. Louis	23	19. Dallas	20
10. Washington, D.C.	44	20. Seattle	26
		Total	957

Though many traditional and cultural factors partly account for the ratings of these cities, the enterprise of a number of leading stores in them has surely contributed to their high standing. The Burrows chain and four active department stores in Cleveland, for example, and the Personal chain, Jordan Marsh, the Old Corner, and the Harvard Co-op, in or near Boston, help give those cities their high standing, despite

[4]In an analysis of the American Book Publishers Council's 1946–47 *Statistical Report,* issued by the Council.

the fact that they have fewer stores and smaller populations than others of lower rank. In New York, both Brentano's and Scribner's carry on large businesses. Doubleday's ten New York stores (part of a national chain of twenty-five) and the book sections in Macy's, Gimbel's, and Bloomingdale's help maintain New York's place at the top of the list. In Chicago, Kroch's stores and the book departments in Marshall Field's and Carson, Pirie, Scott sell many books. Virtually all the rest of the 250 leading American bookstores are located in these twenty cities. The few exceptions are also not in any of the thirty cities in the following list, made by another leading sales manager.

These cities, the first four with more than one hundred thousand people (1940) and the rest with between fifty thousand and one hundred thousand, have no large book outlets. Some have none at all for regular hard-cover books. All are rated poor book towns. This is an expert opinion corrobo-

THIRTY POOR BOOK CITIES AND NUMBER OF BOOKSTORES IN EACH

City	Stores	City	Stores
Kansas City, Kans.	2	Medford, Mass.	0
Gary, Ind.	1	Terre Haute, Ind.	5
Elizabeth, N.J.	1	Jackson, Miss.	4
Somerville, Mass.	0	Covington, Ky.	1
Rockford, Ill.	7	Galveston, Tex.	3
Bayonne, N.J.	0	Chester, Pa.	0
Quincy, Mass.	1	Malden, Mass.	2
Pawtucket, R.I.	2	Union City, N.J.	0
E. St. Louis, Ill.	1	McKeesport, Pa.	2
Springfield, Ill.	2	East Chicago, Ind.	0
Hammond, Ind.	1	Holyoke, Mass.	2
Lakewood, Ohio	1	Pueblo, Colo.	1
Mt. Vernon, N.Y.	1	Highland Park, Mich.	0
Cicero, Ill.	0	Hamilton, Ohio	0
Dearborn, Mich.	1	Hoboken, N.J.	0
		Total	41

rated by others in the industry and based upon sales records or the absence of them.

Next to the name of each city is the number of stores in it, again from the list of 3,041.

The fact that some of these cities neighbor on metropolises like New York, Chicago, and Boston, where comparatively good bookstore service is available, does not greatly improve their standing. It is a truism that where few books are displayed, few are sold, and in these cities few are on display. No one has studied bookstore sales in relation to the proximity of their customers. Library experience indicates that patronage falls markedly as distance from libraries increases, even by a few blocks.[5] The same may well be true of bookstores, with the possible exceptions of the few big stores in the main shopping districts of metropolises. In the cities on this list few people can be near bookstores.

Though it refers to conditions about fifteen years ago, the following statement about the "typical American city" from Robert S. and Helen M. Lynd's *Middletown in Transition* apparently is still largely true: "Middletown is not a book-buying city, though in this respect it is probably not different from other similar midland cities of its size (47,790 in 1933). . . . There is not even a strong book-rental service in the city." The Lynds concluded that the public library supplied the bulk of Middletown's books, even the rental service being "performed by the 'new book' rental library in the public library."[6]

Since the distortions in the American Book Publishers Council's 1946–47 statistics on the distribution of book sales

[5]There is interesting information on this point in another Public Library Inquiry publication, Bernard Berelson, *The Library's Public*, New York, Columbia University Press, 1949. See especially the section "Residence" in chap. ii.

[6]Robert S. Lynd and Helen M. Lynd, *Middletown in Transition*, New York, Harcourt, 1937, p. 252n.

are much less grave for regions than for cities or states, with the caveats noted on pages 94–95 above, sales by regions are presented here.

The regions are not those of the United States census reports, but of the Publishers Council and reflect more or less accurately the normal boundaries of trade publishers' sales territories. Figures by states grouped in these regions are given in Appendix B; they can be rearranged in any other regional summary. "Publishers' sales" in the second column are direct sales (to bookstores and individuals, but not to wholesalers) as reported by twenty trade houses.

Region	Percentage of 20 Publishers' 1946 Direct Sales	Percentage of U.S. Population (1946 Estimates)
Northeastern	42.4	26.5
East Central	19.2	20.4
Southeastern	11.1	21.3
West Central	11.2	19.3
Western	16.1	12.5
TOTALS (=100 PERCENT)	$30,000,000	139,893,406

EXPANDING THE TRADE   The thirty American cities listed above with populations of fifty thousand or more are probably not the only ones of that size where few new books are sold. Why cannot or why do not such cities support bookstores? Studies seeking the answer to this question would cast new light on American cultural and business life. By showing what social changes must be made before books can be sold successfully in these cities or what new types of sales effort can exploit already favorable social situations, such studies would be especially valuable to publishers and booksellers.

Trade book business cannot be expanded steadily and permanently simply by working over the same old ground. Yet new ground seems to respond very reluctantly to it. The sales manager for one of the biggest regular trade publishers said early in 1948 that while there are now "some 50 percent more outlets than eight years ago," this expansion has been "more of the same"; it has been "largely in big cities already supplied with outlets. There has been no expansion in the South at all with the exception of Texas. Growth has been more in concentration in good places than any extensive development." He noted that the "biggest expansion regionally has been on the West coast," but in Boston, St. Louis, Washington, New York, and other older metropolises there are also new accounts.[7]

Trade publishers welcome new outlets almost anywhere, and wholesalers particularly are helpful to new stores in smaller towns. Yet the continuing vigor of the metropolises has focused the industry's major expansionist effort in them. The Book Distribution Committee of the American Book Publishers Council has been most intent upon getting more big city department stores to install book sections.

Even this effort, however, has recently, if only temporarily, been thwarted. Rising book prices and declining sales since 1946 have caused many department stores to reconsider their book business in terms of the value of the space it takes up. Some department stores have stopped selling books; as for others taking books on, Albert Leventhal, of Simon & Schuster, who is in charge of this part of the committee's work, reported at the council's annual meeting in May, 1948, that "the opening of new outlets for the sale of books during the past year proved to be an extremely tough job." About seventy-five department stores had been contacted, and "most showed no interest."[8]

The committee's setback in its most favored project has caused it to intensify its efforts elsewhere. It has sought with some success to get the 650 college stores at schools with one

[7]In interview with author.
[8]*Publishers' Weekly*, May 29, 1948.

thousand or more students to stock new trade books. It has interested more music stores in music books, sporting goods stores in sport books, religious stores in religious books, and so forth.

The council's continuing efforts represent a centralized attack on the "outlets" problem unprecedented in the industry. As yet this attack is too new for the measurement of permanent gains. One important consequence, however—it will be called a gain or a loss depending on the point of view—may be a still greater emphasis upon best sellers. Already they are the major concern of most department stores and chains of bookstores. Though such outlets often carry a wide range of books, the bulk of their business is in a small number of heavily advertised titles. Their salespeople, among whom turnover is high and who in department stores are often drafted from sections alien to books, usually are unacquainted even with current titles and scarcely able to sell unfamiliar ones at all. This is also true of college stores, where salespeople are likely to be least experienced and turnover to be highest.

Cheney's *Survey*, in 1930–31, showed that department stores even then accounted for almost 38 percent of all bookstore sales; today the figure is considerably higher, but there is no agreement on how much. In many cities the book section of a department store is now the leading bookstore. Department stores, after all, sell books fast—or not at all. They generally pay promptly and are more reliable financially than many independent booksellers. Most department stores insist on buying directly from the publishers; they feel that they get better service this way and hence can control their buying and their inventories more closely. Moreover, department stores do not like to bear any part of the middleman's (wholesaler's) profits. Though some of them have curtailed their buying since 1947, many still buy leading titles in large quantities, and all expect the best discounts. Since publishers usually can offer

higher discounts than can wholesalers (and yet lower discounts than they must give to wholesalers), the publishers get
most of this profitable business and want more of it.

THE LONG VIEW   Yet it may be as shortsighted for publishers, for a slightly higher net price and other inducements,
to encourage department and chain stores and other big accounts to by-pass wholesalers as it is for publishers, in however few instances, to compete with wholesalers in selling
trade books to public, school, and college libraries. Raymond
C. Harwood, of Harper's, said early in 1948: "Any attempt of
book publishers to secure better distribution of their product
must inevitably include the examination of the adequacy of
present jobbing [wholesaling] arrangements."[9] If these "arrangements" function poorly, it is partly because the wholesalers are ordinarily left with only the poorer accounts. Even
were they of a mind to do so, they are given scant opportunity to build up strong regional dealers around strong regional
distribution centers—with modern warehouses, prompt delivery service, and constant and close stock controls.

These features can be found in the wholesaling arrangements of virtually all other industries selling in the national
market. Closest to home, they can be found in paper-bound
books. In that segment of the book industry the wholesaler is
supreme in his region. The publishers' salesmen serve mainly
as sales "engineers"; they instruct dealers on promotional
schemes, on how to sell, on what to feature; frequently they
check dealers' displays and dealers' stock. But except from a
few large and adamant accounts, they take no orders from retailers.

Such an arrangement is mandatory in an industry in which
each company's survival depends largely upon its ability to keep

[9]In an analysis of the American Book Publishers Council's 1946–47 *Statistical Report*, issued by the council.

huge numbers of books moving in tens of thousands of outlets. For publishers of original trade books, different sales objectives would have to be defined. But even now a modern
regional warehousing and distribution system would insure
dealers against running out of titles still heavily in demand. It
would enable them quickly to replenish low stocks of other
active titles and to cut down the time required to fill special
orders. Such a system would speed up the flow of all books to
the consumer, raise almost every dealer's turnover, ease the returns and remainders problems by making it easier to shift
books selling poorly in some areas to regions where the demand is greater. Most important, such a system, working in
harmony and not in competition with the publishers, would
probably stimulate the opening of new and efficient bookstores and help the better going ones to grow.

Among trade publishers only Macmillan has regional warehouses, in New York, Boston, Chicago, Dallas, and San Fran-
cisco, but most of their work is with the firm's school and
college textbooks. Among wholesalers, only American News
has such warehouses, but these are said to be weak in many
types of stock. If American News cannot improve its service
and if the other wholesalers cannot extend theirs, other publishers, individually or in groups, may well consider emulating
Macmillan by opening their own warehouses. Large firms may
do more; their own warehouses may be made into service agencies for their own retail chains, on the model of Doubleday's
stores. This would only be in keeping with trends in other industries, where manufacturing and retailing have become
parts of the same integrated operation.

SHORT VIEW AIDS   Regional warehousing and integrated retail distribution have been talked of in the book industry for
decades, but must still be looked upon as goals for the distant
future. In the meantime, many penny-wise (not necessarily

dollar-foolish) short-term measures have been taken to improve distribution through channels now available.

The council's Book Distribution Committee, for example, has helped get publishers and booksellers to adopt uniform returns policies (there is still a good deal of opposition to these on both sides) and machinery for handling other long disputed issues. It has had experts study improved retailing methods and has issued brochures on them: two so far published are *Direct-Mail Selling for Booksellers*, by L. Howard Moss, Jr., and *Book Windows That Sell*, by Michael Gross. It is working on schemes for enlarging co-operative publisher-bookseller advertising in local areas.

The committee's major project in 1948 was the Ohio Plan, an unprecedented experiment to test intensively (in a "good book state") "all the ideas of the several subcommittees" of the Book Distribution group. New selling techniques for retailers and publishers are expected to result from the experiment; it is also expected to clarify the value of older practices and lead to the discarding of useless ones, however traditional. In Ohio, with the experiment in progress, book sales rose appreciably; whether this was due to successful application of generally useful ideas or simply to the enthusiasm of those engaged in the tests will not be known until the general ideas are set forth and tried elsewhere under normal conditions.

Perhaps as important to booksellers as any other services are those of the American Booksellers Association, six of which may be noted: (1) Publication of the ABA monthly *Bulletin*. (2) Compilation of the annual *Book Buyers' Handbook*, which contains among other things the discount and returns policies of all publishers. The first *Handbook* was issued in 1947; it and succeeding issues are free to ABA members; $4 to others. For nonmembers who buy books in quantity it is probably worth the price many times over. (3) Distribution of the annual *Basic Book List* of most active backlist titles. This is a useful buying guide. The first list, of about twenty-three hundred titles, was issued in 1946 and included, unfortunately, some titles out of print; later lists have been larger and more carefully made up. (4) Development of the "packaged book shop," available in prefabricated parts for those opening new shops and as a model for redesigning others. (5) Development, in the spring of 1947, of the "Give-a-Book-Certificate" plan, by which tokens purchased in a participant store may be redeemed in any other in any part of the country for any book or books of equal value (the English have long had a similar scheme). (6) Implementation of a plan to fight the book clubs with their own fire.

The booksellers' major complaint against the clubs is price cutting, which is effected by lower cash prices and offers of free books. The booksellers hold publishers partly responsible for this, because of their low plate rentals (royalties) to the clubs and their unwillingness to lower bookstore prices on club selections. The booksellers themselves, according to Gilbert Goodkind, executive secretary of the ABA, have planned "to lease plates from various publishers from time to time. Using these plates we will print, bind, distribute, and to some degree advertise the title."[10]

Early in 1948 the ABA asked publishers to submit their "customary royalty fees" for the leasing of plates to those who guarantee from ten thousand to one hundred thousand copies. None complied. The first title sought by the ABA was Churchill's *The Gathering Storm;* its publisher, Houghton Mifflin, rejected the ABA bid. Subsequently Harper's refused a bid for Betty Smith's *Tomorrow Will Be Better,* and Doubleday one for Eisenhower's *Crusade in Europe.* In the meantime the Federal Trade Commission has been re-examining the whole problem of free-book offers as a competitive weapon.

[10]New York *Herald Tribune,* February 1, 1948.

Court fights over publishers' alleged discrimination against
the ABA and over the clubs' alleged unfair trade practices
have been threatened, but some of the issues were expected to
be settled in less militant fashion after the Book-of-the-Month
Club greatly curtailed its "Alternates" plan, and Harry Scherman announced, as reported in *Publishers' Weekly*, July 31,
1948, "We have not the slightest objection if any publisher
lowers the retail price of a selection, in order to make it the
same as our price to members." The next move seems to be
the publishers'.

The major wholesalers also have short-view aids for booksellers (and libraries) using their services. Among the most
valued of these are the free, monthly buying guides: American News Company's *American News of Books*, Baker and
Taylor's *The Retail Bookseller*, and McClurg's *Book News*.
Other important guides are the American Library Association's *Book List* and the varied information in the *Library
Journal*. For an annual fee the Virginia Kirkus Bookshop
Service supplies booksellers (and libraries) with regular semi-
monthly and other special bulletins, all containing up-to-the-
minute prepublication critical information very useful in selling and even more important in buying trade books.

Publishers' Weekly, the files of which make up the only
good history of the industry, each week has very useful business information for booksellers and libraries, and for more
than seventy-five years has been an open forum for book-
seller-publisher discussions of industry problems.

CATALOGUE, COUPON, AND CIRCULAR   But the short-run
efforts of the American Book Publishers Council, the ABA,
and other agencies cannot extend the bookstore market appreciably; they cannot help booksellers reach very many of
the sixty million Americans believed to be outside the regular
bookstore system.

There is, however, another system through which this great market can be tapped. There are about forty-three thousand post offices in the United States; through them goes virtually every kind of merchandise, including books. The exploiters of mail-order facilities range from giants such as Sears, Roebuck and Montgomery Ward, through the major and minor book clubs, to the smallest publisher who ever tried a direct-mail campaign or a coupon advertisement.

Largely through its catalogue, which goes annually to more than seven million selected consumers, Sears sells about as great a dollar volume of books as the entire trade department of the largest trade publisher. Ward's volume is about 75 percent of Sears'. Both do most of their business in Bibles, religious books, and low-priced juveniles. Cheap technical and self-improvement books and hard-cover reprints account for almost all the rest. Each sells a few current best sellers.

The bookstores do not worry about Sears' and Ward's mail-order business; the stores themselves do well enough with Bibles and do not like to stock most of the other books sold by the big mail-order houses. Moreover, the bookstores acknowledge that they are largely inaccessible to Sears' and Ward's many rural customers.

The stores are more concerned about the direct-mail selling and coupon advertising of trade publishers. Though the latter use the mails to sell only a few titles a year, these are almost always new and expensive ones or stable backlist items that are more likely than are Sears' and Ward's books to result in large sales for bookstores.

Many case histories show, however, that publishers' direct-mail or coupon advertising considerably increases the bookstore sale of titles so advertised. Direct-mail or coupon campaigns draw thousands of new buyers into the bookstores; where there are no bookstores, the publisher, naturally, makes the sales—but this cannot hurt and, indeed, may often help the booksellers.

The evidence for this is elaborate and conclusive. Two parts of the supporting argument were stated in *Publishers' Weekly*, March 20, 1948, by Victor O. Schwab in "How Mail-Order Advertising by Publishers Helps Booksellers," the sequel to an article quoted early in this chapter.

If a mail order advertisement, [he said] pulls orders from 1/10 of 1 percent of the circulation of the publication in which it appears, it is doing very well. . . . Yet this mail-order result enables the advertiser to EXPOSE the selling talk about the book to 200,000 people [or whatever the circulation of a given medium]. In other words, even though only 200 people buy the book by mail, 199,800 additional people have been exposed to the advertisement—an advertisement which may be merely *part* of an extensive advertising campaign that would never have been run at all unless it could bring back a satisfactory part of its cost in direct business.

Schwab's second point is that "by 'sampling' the book *nation-wide* more quickly and more widely through the more sizable advertising appropriation which the result of mail-order may make financially possible," direct-mail and coupon campaigns get an unusually fast start for " '*word-of-mouth*' advertising." "Even when the initial sale of the book has been consummated by mail," Schwab says, "if the thoroughly satisfied reader of that book recommends it highly to others *they* purchase it, wherever possible, at the retailers. This factor is clearly and unmistakably reflected" in the following example of a book which at the time the tabulation was made was "still selling 1,000 copies per week in the bookstores at full price." This was a "book on personality development," for which $106,652 had been "expended for couponed mail-order advertising." This campaign accounted for "mail-order sales" of 131,635 copies. At the same time, only $980 had been "expended for non-couponed advertising for bookstore sale," yet the bookstore sale of the original, full-price edition had already reached 836,493 copies, and a paper-bound edition had reached 2,013,431 copies.

Schwab's article contains a number of other convincing examples. Another advertising agency reports the following experience with a book that had been sold widely in its regular edition and also in a dollar edition, but had apparently run its course in the stores. A coupon advertisement was placed in *Life* for $12,500. This almost immediately brought the publisher more than twenty-five thousand dollars, and after a few weeks more than thirty-four thousand dollars, in direct sales. In the meantime the revived bookstore sale of the original edition was so great that the publisher, in a short period after the advertisement was run, had more than fifteen thousand dollars in orders from this market. Throughout, the dollar edition of the book had been on sale in the stores.

Selling individual titles by mail is costly; with few exceptions books priced under three dollars cannot be sold profitably that way. This may explain why direct-mail and coupon advertisements, though apparently geared to reach rural markets, do best in urban areas where more cash is available. However, Robert West Howard, former editor of *Pathfinder* and the *Farm Journal*, believes that the publishers' failure to reach rural markets is a result, not of pricing, but of editorial policies.

In an article in *Publishers' Weekly*, May 22, 1948, entitled rather optimistically "The Billion Dollar Furrow," Howard said that while "estimates of current [rural family] expenditures [for books] ranged from $1 to $10," the "average rural family can afford to spend annually from $15 per family per year in Mississippi, lowest income state, to $50 in Utah, New York, and the Corn Belt." All told, Howard estimates that this market of sixty million people, "if researched properly, should gross [for publishers] an average of $400,000,000 within three years, and rise steadily to an average of $1,000,-000,000 a year." A careful selection of books would help publishers capture this magnificent (if real) market, he said; he also recommended a "semi-final review, in manuscript, of books intended for the rural audience by a review board composed of men and women familiar with rural America."

If convinced that this market were available to them, many publishers and authors would issue books for it and would gladly yield to such a review. It may be, however, that if this market is as big as Howard thinks it is, entirely new publishers with new methods and new aims could do best in it. Attempts by present trade publishers to supply it adequately would probably mean abandoning their present largely urban market and the bookstores that serve it.

ADVERTISING THE LIST   Though all new books issued by regular trade publishers are said to be advertised, for most of them this means only a line or two in publishers' announcements to the booksellers, mainly in *Publishers' Weekly*. Others, in groups of five or six or ten or more, may simply be listed once or twice in advertisements in the daily and especially the Sunday book editions of the New York *Times* and the New York *Herald Tribune*. These papers, according to reliable estimates, carry at least 60 percent of all trade book advertising. Their Sunday sections, to be sure, are read in all parts of the country; the Sunday New York *Times Book Review* has a circulation of two hundred and fifty thousand in eleven thousand "cities, towns, villages and hamlets" outside the metropolitan area. Only books with big anticipated or actual sales, and a few others to satisfy their authors, get display space in these papers or in those of seven or eight other "principal cities"—the more exceptional the sales, of course, the larger and more frequent the advertisements and the more numerous the media.

Most of the rest of trade book advertising is restricted to local or other special promotion for books with local or special appeals and to advertisements in book-reviewing magazines, such as the *Saturday Review of Literature*, the *New Republic*, the *Nation*, *Harper's*, the *Atlantic*, and the *New Yorker*. Some small literary and scholarly periodicals also carry a few trade book advertisements.

Space in the huge-circulation "slick-paper" magazines is too costly for most books. Best sellers, especially if they have been or are to be made into movies, are advertised occasionally in them. So are a few of the books sold directly to consumers by coupon advertisements including major book club selections, premiums, and dividends.

Thus, aside from paper-bound books on display almost everywhere and self-improvement and inspirational literature offered by direct mail, out of the thousands of new books issued each year by trade publishers only the topmost best sellers and major book club titles come to the attention of most Americans who read. The book clubs' titles, whether dividends, premiums or selections, are likely to be the most widely seen of all.

BOOK CLUB PROMOTION   The Book-of-the-Month Club says that "considerably less than 10 percent of our advertising expenditures is in so-called book media."[11] In 1946 this "less than 10 percent" was more than $250,000, a figure well above that for most trade publishers' annual expenditures for all their advertising. The club's 1946 budget allotted an additional $728,332 for space in nationally circulated "slick" magazines and another two million dollars for the many special projects that make up most of book club promotion.

[11]*Publishers' Weekly*, May 24, 1947.

Some of these projects were summarized by a Book-of-the-Month Club spokesman in *Publishers' Weekly*, May 24, 1947. Since then, activities and expenditures have been cut down, but not so much as to alter the implications of this summary:

We distribute almost 950,000 copies of the Book-of-the-Month Club *News* each month. 7,000 of them go to libraries and institutions which have asked for them. . . . In addition to our display advertising and our distribution of the *News*, the Club sent out something over 12,000,000 mailing pieces last year. Regardless of the offer, they claim the recipient's interest for books, for book ownership.

We furnish a 15-minute radio script about books weekly to 540 radio stations in all parts of the country. An additional 250 of these radio scripts are sent upon request to schools and colleges and libraries, largely for use in classroom work.

We supply 1,500 newspapers regularly with a book review column called "Reading & Writing." We also supply 1,600 women's clubs monthly with a 30-minute book-news letter.

We sponsor "The Author Meets the Critics" program which is now to be on a national hook-up. . . . We have sponsored The New Friends of Music program, during the intermission of which Dr. Canby discussed current books.

This barrage, like the Literary Guild's advertising, which approaches that of the Book-of-the-Month Club in volume and is almost as varied, is focused on getting and holding members. The bulk of it plays up the attractive free books for joiners and describes in glowing terms the current cut-price selection and perhaps one or two earlier bargains still available. These few titles catch the full glare of club advertising.

In the Guild's promotion and that of most other clubs, these are the only titles named. In the Book-of-the-Month Club *News*, however, as many as one hundred new books are sometimes mentioned. These are not merely listed; virtually all of them carry comment, ranging from two pages to a few lines, all favorable, of course, since these are books recommended by the club. Many of them are also mentioned in the club's other releases, which may also boost sales.

Part of these sales fall to the Book-of-the-Month Club, which (like most other clubs) not only distributes selections and recommended books, but does a large mail-order business in all trade titles. But bookstores also, wherever they may be found, often benefit from this publicity, at least in sales of these particular titles. The announcement that a book is to be a major club's selection usually (though sometimes mistakenly) leads the publisher to increase his own initial printing and the booksellers to enlarge their initial orders. For books not selected by major clubs yet mentioned in their publicity, considerable impetus may also be given to bookstore sales.

BOOK CLUB SALES AND THE BOOKSTORE MARKET   Many hold that book club publicity, by focusing so much of American book buying upon a few titles, hurts the sales of the rest and hence the business of bookstores trying to sell a wide range of books. Lovell Thompson, of Houghton Mifflin, took this stand in the *Saturday Review of Literature*, March 1, 1947.

It is often pointed out that a book-club adoption increases the sale of the adopted title, but it is usually forgotten that the publishers give up part of their market by yielding to the book clubs a market which they could exploit directly. . . . Though the book clubs increase the market for individual titles, they decrease the original publisher's market for all titles. The net result is more books sold, but fewer books sold by the publisher.

Others go still further; they argue that increasingly bookstore sales even of club selections are being hurt because of the cut prices usually offered by the clubs. An illustration was given in *Publishers' Weekly*, December 11, 1948.

One of our better small bookstores began to solicit advance orders for the Eisenhower book as soon as it was announced, and ran up a list of orders for publication delivery of 43 copies at $5.00. When the Book-of-the-Month Club edition at $3.75 was announced, 20 orders were canceled.

This is not a good business situation for anyone. No one can blame the customer for buying at $3.75 plus premium rights, but it does not take much imagination to picture the deflated feeling of the bookseller who had spent more time and money in getting the now 24 [sic] remaining orders than the total sale could possibly warrant. And if another pre-publication offer is made later by the dealer, at least 40 percent of the shop's best customers will be cynical as to the shop's usefulness to them. An increasingly wide public is unfortunately becoming aware that the marketing of new books is in a confused state of price competition.

These arguments are not new, and club spokesmen have not let them go unanswered. A Book-of-the-Month Club executive, for example, wrote in *Publishers' Weekly*, May 24, 1947:

To suppose that all of the 12,000,000 persons who are reached by our mailing pieces, or the millions of others who read our advertising, or any considerable number of them immediately subscribe as Club members is, of course, ridiculous. We are satisfied if one percent of those who receive circulars respond, and an infinitely smaller percentage of those who read the advertisements, but the other 99 percent of the 12,000,000 persons who have been circularized, and the many more millions who have read our advertisements and are subject to our general promotions have been exposed to book publicity, and the record shows indisputably that this is reflected in additional sales in bookstores. . . .

Nor do all those who do respond directly to book club advertising continue indefinitely as subscribers. They join, they buy, they read a certain number of our books, they are exposed to regular periodic information about books over an extended period of time. Many of them unquestionably acquire the habit of reading, the desire for book ownership, in other words, they become

habitual book buyers, but for one reason or another they do not
remain members. As an average for book clubs generally I would
say that 50 percent cancel each year. During the life of the
[Book-of-the-Month] Club 2,700,000 subscribers have canceled.
It is safe to say, I think, that a great many of them still buy books,
but from bookstores.

All told, it has been estimated that five million persons who
once belonged to book clubs are no longer members. Some
probably were so discouraged by the low (or high) quality
of club selections that they will seldom buy current books
again; others may have found, after a year or so of membership, that they had all the books they cared to own; a third
group, given gift memberships, may have had no desire to re-
new them; a fourth, using club selections as furniture, may
have had no more shelf space. By far the largest group is believed to be of those no longer able to afford to buy four
books a year no matter how many others are offered free.

Taken together, these groups must account for most of the
five million ex-members. Despite the Book-of-the Month Club
spokesman's views, few of them are likely to become good
customers of bookstores even when stores are accessible. How
many of the others may become active bookstore customers?
Here, too, there are divergent opinions, but no convincing
data.

Remarkably enough, about five hundred bookstores and
book sections of department stores sell memberships in the
Literary Guild and the Book-of-the-Month Club. They find
this good business because of the commissions paid by the
clubs; they also find that more than 80 percent of the people
who buy club memberships had never before purchased books
in the stores. Some buy non-club books as well as memberships; others are suspected of going from store to store and
signing up for the clubs simply to get the free books handed
out by them.

The extent of this racket has not been estimated; since the stores and the clubs still do this joint business, it cannot be too widespread. Yet it has still to be shown that club members buy many non-club books; as for ex-members, probably the best test so far was that conducted in 1947, when "on behalf of ABA bookstores" Doubleday tried "large mailings" on three books to former members of its clubs. "Sales results proved to be nowhere near the amount required to reimburse the very large investment made by Doubleday, Garden City, and the other cooperating publishers." Milo Sutliff, then in charge of all Doubleday's clubs, said that "the results of these mailings offer further proof that the type of person who will enroll in a book club is not the type of person who is likely to make a regular bookstore customer. The best promotion results for stores can be obtained by careful building up of the store's own customer lists."[12]

THE BOOK CLUB MARKET   Of the three million members in American book clubs at the end of 1947 (the number has since decreased), approximately 80 percent were in three clubs: the Literary Guild (900,000), the Book-of-the-Month Club (770,000) and the Dollar Book Club (700,000). About 10 percent were in the People's Book Club (300,000), 5 percent in the Fiction Book Club (150,000), 2 percent in the Book Find Club (60,000). The remaining 3 percent were thinly strewn over the remaining seventy to eighty clubs.

Only the Book-of-the-Month Club has made public its membership history, which is shown in the following table along with the total number of books, including selections, dividends, and bonuses, distributed annually by that club and its annual advertising and promotion expenditures (the latter figures include the cost of book gifts to new members). The number of members is as of December 31 each year, except

[12]*ABA Bulletin,* February, 1948.

for April, 1946, when the club reached its all-time peak of 918,000.[13]

MEMBERS OF AND BOOKS DISTRIBUTED BY THE BOOK-OF-THE-MONTH CLUB

Year	Members, As of December 31	Number of Books Distributed	Advertising Expenditures[a]
1926	46,539	232,389	. . .
1927	60,058	641,978	. . .
1928	94,690	867,390	. . .
1929	110,588	986,044	. . .
1930	93,660	843,300	. . .
1931	82,248	892,235	. . .
1932	88,025	973,356	. . .
1933	94,739	963,338	. . .
1934	93,070	949,828	. . .
1935	137,019	1,197,440	. . .
1936	195,785	1,613,999	. . .
1937	246,337	2,327,449	$664,823.30
1938	282,300	2,821,301	674,946.99
1939	362,585	3,360,217	898,970.29
1940	404,451	3,768,667	793,306.32
1941	517,785	4,858,702	1,293,123.16
1942	584,773	5,932,203	1,367,760.99
1943	633,455	6,765,739	1,051,275.95
1944	636,422	6,965,176	832,776.37
1945	767,622	7,860,258	1,337,925.80
1946 (April)	918,000	. . .	. . .
1946	889,305	11,412,647	2,950,848.62
1947	776,849	11,089,864	2,539,500.00
1948[b]	600,000[b]	. . .	. . .

[a]No advertising data are available for 1926–36.

[b]This figure is from *Publishers' Weekly*, February 19, 1949, p. 976, which reported that "the club had 503,283 members on January 26, 1949, in the United States, excluding Canadian and bookseller accounts (these two categories, *PW* understands, would bring the total somewhat under 600,000)."

[13]The table is from the Prospectus of the Book-of-the-Month Club, March, 1947, except for the 1947 figures which are from *Publishers' Weekly*, November 27, 1948, and the 1948 figure which is from *Publishers' Weekly*, February 19, 1949.

In 1946 the Book-of-the-Month Club guaranteed publishers and authors a minimum sale of 333,333 copies, which at 30 cents a copy for single selections came to $100,000 and at 20 cents a copy for dual selections, to $66,667. Actual sales of selections that year averaged about 460,000 copies. In April, 1948, the club's guarantee was reduced to $80,000 for single and $50,000 for dual selections on minimum sales of about 250,000 copies. Actual sales probably decreased at least in the same proportion.

Most book clubs, lest they disclose their best marketing areas to competitors, try to keep secret the geographical breakdowns of their membership. However, information has been made available on the basis of which the following approximate regional distribution in the United States (about 5 or 6 percent of their members live abroad, mainly in Canada) of the 1947 membership of the larger clubs has been constructed. It would be enlightening to know what portion of book club members live in the twenty best book cities listed earlier in this chapter and how many in the thirty poor book cities named, but such information cannot be obtained.

The regions used in this table are made up of the same states as in the table on page 98 showing publishers' sales to bookstores and individuals; the breakdown of club membership by states is given in Appendix B.

Region	Percentage of Book Club Membership	Percentage of U.S. Population 1946 Estimates
Northeastern	33.8	26.5
East Central	21.5	20.4
Southeastern	15.3	21.3
West Central	13.4	19.3
Western	16.0	12.5
TOTAL (=100 PERCENT)	a	139,893,406

aThe actual membership total on which these percentages are based is confidential.

Sear's People's Book Club, Doubleday's Family Book Club, and some other smaller ones probably have most of their members in rural areas. Memberships in the Literary Guild and in the Dollar Book Club are sold to rural members (and to others) through Montgomery Ward's catalogue. Coupon advertisements in national magazines no doubt get additional rural members for them and for other big clubs. Yet there are no public over-all figures to offset the pervasive and accepted opinion in the book industry that most club members are in cities of twenty-five thousand or more. The book club market, generally speaking, is taken to be an urban one.

This may reflect the clubs' failure to reach the large rural population not otherwise brought within the ken of current literature. But it may reflect, too, the weakness of the American bookstore system. If the clubs are strongest where the bookstores have their greatest opportunity, it may be concluded that the stores have missed masses of people who make that opportunity seem so great. They may have lost customers to the clubs because of the latter's impressive price and premium inducements; yet it may be that because they themselves now generally make so much of best sellers and even of major book club selections they are especially vulnerable to book club competition.

To reverse this situation, to restore the stores to the condition in which their range of titles is their strength, and to restore the book buying community to an appreciation of this strength, may well take a cultural revolution; without one, the department stores, already dominant among book "outlets" in many places, will probably become stronger still. These stores have their own uses for best sellers and club selections; to compete with them, independent booksellers even now often must follow their lead.

A NOTE ON RENTALS   One of the impressive aspects of American book publishing, although some European countries excel the United States in this, is the great number and variety of titles issued each year.[14] But the infinitesimal market for all but a few of these titles is depressing. Book renting scarcely improves the record of book buying.

Not all of the better American bookstores have rental libraries, but those that do, usually have the best ones. These stores often place in their libraries many of the current books, which they also buy for sale; the range of their rental books may be as wide as the wants of their most demanding customers. About half of the 3,041 stores noted above also have rental libraries, their quality, no doubt, varying with the size and quality of the stores.

There are probably more than fifty thousand other rental libraries in the United States, not counting those itinerants who visit offices and homes with bags of rental books and whose business, some say, is "surprisingly large," whatever that may mean. Most of the fifty thousand libraries are controlled by ten big chains. The best libraries are said to be those run by the Walden Book Company; the largest chain is probably that of the American Lending Library Company, which has approximately ten thousand "outlets."

Best selling fiction and detective stories account for most of the business of these libraries; detective stories alone gross more than half the total. About one fourth of all new fiction published each year, or approximately three hundred titles, are detective stories; rental libraries buy roughly 80 percent of all copies. Each copy may be rented as many as sixty times over a period of three or four years. The American Lending Library Company buys only two or three hundred copies of rental staples; these normally are put in the chain's best libraries, replacing older stock, which in turn replaces still older stock at the next level of the chain's outlets. Other chains also start their books in metropolitan libraries and work them down to hinterland markets.

[14]See Appendix B.

If publishers' sales of the three hundred new detective titles each year average three thousand copies at a net price of $1.00 to $1.50 (depending on retail price and discount), income from this business must be more than a million dollars annually. Publishers' gross from other books circulated by rental libraries must be at least as much, making about two million dollars in all.

5

TRADE PUBLISHING AND
THE PUBLIC LIBRARIES

SERVING public—and school and college—libraries is only a small part of most trade publishers' activities, a part, indeed, which, even now, when library book budgets are growing and publishers' profits from other markets are shrinking, some publishers neglect almost entirely. Because of the traditional difficulties in selling books to public libraries and collecting money from them, some publishers believe they actually profit from avoiding this market. No public libraries, however, can profit from neglecting the publishers. Each of the latter's decisions, whether in finance, editing, production, or distribution, must deeply affect library action and library policy. The quality of trade books and the terms on which they may be had are of overwhelming importance to all public libraries, even if public library buying often seems comparatively unimportant to many trade publishers.

In 1948 all American libraries spent an estimated thirty-two million dollars for books and periodicals; the public libraries' share of this was about thirteen million dollars (compared to $10,400,000 in 1945[1]). Somewhat more than 10 percent was for periodicals; 85 to 90 percent of the remainder, or about ten million dollars, was for trade books.[2] Of this, at most two

[1]Willard O. Mishoff and Emery M. Foster, *Public Library Statistics, 1944–45,* Office of Education, Bulletin 1947, No. 12, Washington, D.C., Government Printing Office, 1947, p. 13.

[2]The estimated 1948 total expenditures are from *Publishers' Weekly,* January 15, 1949. The percentages used in these tabulations are based mainly on information gathered for the Public Library Inquiry by Watson O'D. Pierce.

million dollars went directly to trade publishers; the rest went to wholesalers and a few retailers for books purchased by them from trade publishers for about $6,400,000, making the publishers' total income from public libraries in 1948 approximately $8,400,000. Thus, of regular trade publishers' ninety to one hundred million dollars volume in 1948 (exclusive of income from subsidiary rights) approximately 9 percent was from public libraries. For adult books alone, the figure would be at most six million dollars, or between 6 and 7 percent. Some publishers of paper-bound books began selling to public libraries in recent years, but income from such sales has been very small.

Though these over-all figures for library buying are available for 1948, the latest year for which detailed breakdowns of library budgets are available is 1945, when, as has been said, the total spent for books and periodicals was about 20 percent below the figures for the later year.[3] The 1945 figures show that a few library systems, notably those in New York City, Chicago, Boston, Cleveland, and Detroit and the county systems in California, are large book buyers, though none spent more than $250,000 for trade books that year. In only eighteen states did total 1945 public-library expenditures for trade books come to an estimated $100,000 or more; for adult books alone, this amount was spent in only thirteen states.

In 1945 there were 7,408 public library systems in the United States (most of them consisting of but one library), of which 5,799 reported their total annual operating budgets to the United States Office of Education. Of these, 2,221 had less than $1,000 for all expenditures (including books); 1,916 others had $1,000 to $3,999. Practically all the 1,709 public library systems that did not report also fell into one of these groups, making a total of 5,846 systems, or about 80 percent,

[3] See *Public Library Statistics, 1944-45*.

serving at least 10 to 15 percent of the population; their book purchases, even in the aggregate, could scarcely have amounted to much.

This general poverty makes it easy to imagine a vigorous trade publishing industry without public library buying at all; abroad, one may see trade book industries that have thrived virtually without public library aid. A public library system without a trade publishing industry, however, can scarcely be conceived.

PUBLIC LIBRARY BUYING   Of course, money is not everything. It is often said that when retail booksellers had most of the public library business, however small, they were able to carry more varied stocks than they do today and that library business was the best brake on best sellerism in the stores. From this the inference may be drawn that if public libraries should again buy from independent booksellers, the resistance of the latter to best sellerism would grow stronger and a large and growing market for serious literature would reappear. This would spur the younger serious writers and the trade publishers to a renewed interest in serious work.

The assumptions in this argument, however, are not altogether acceptable. That independent bookstores push best sellers harder today than ever before is likely. This may be due to their loss of public library business, but there are other plausible reasons: the growing competition of department stores; the unprecedented promotion of a few titles by publishers, book clubs, and movie companies; the heightened attractiveness of such books to publishers competing for subsidiary income. A more nebulous factor may be the increase of faddism among American readers.

This appraisal of the effects of public library buying also overlooks the libraries' own tendency to buy and circulate the most popular books. Best sellers, whether purchased from local dealers, wholesalers, or publishers, have usually been most in demand by adult and adolescent card holders and most generously supplied by the libraries. Indeed, many public libraries select their adult books from best seller lists or from advertisements and reviews featuring candidates for such lists.

In 1931, when many retailers still had public library business, Cheney wrote:

Each year the publishers issue hundreds of nonfiction titles which they believe to be of significance and which they feel sure will be in enough demand from the libraries to make publication safe from danger of loss. Each year the publishers realize disappointments—and the result is that some excellent works are discouraged and the public is deprived of access to them.[4]

Since then discouragement of such works has increased. "This is a library book; it will have a good library sale" is still heard at publishers' editorial meetings, but far less frequently than heretofore. After years of disappointment some publishers have learned (though without having any exact knowledge) that most libraries do not and, indeed, cannot buy many serious titles and that those that buy a few cannot buy many copies of them. Moreover, even the best possible library sale of a serious book can no longer cover more than a small fraction of production and other costs.

Juveniles account for more than 40 percent of the entire circulation of most public libraries, and from 30 to 40 percent of many libraries' total annual expenditure for books. Some libraries, part of or closely associated with school systems, spend 60 to 70 percent of their entire book budgets on juveniles. On technical and professional books most libraries spend nothing, and few spend more than 10 percent of their book funds. If the bookstores were to reclaim their former

[4]Cheney, *Economic Survey of the Book Industry, 1930–1931*, pp. 313–14.

share of juvenile and technical and professional volume at old-time discounts of 10 to 20 percent (and no one explains how they may do this) the only important result would be that the libraries, because of lower discounts, would pay higher prices and buy even fewer such books. If the bookstores, at the old discount rates, also reclaimed their lost business in general adult books, the catastrophe would be even greater.

If retailers, on the other hand, were to try to recapture public library business by competing in discounts with wholesalers and publishers, they would probably become insolvent. Most of them have a hard enough time staying in business when they sell books at full price; they scarcely can give time, energy, or capital to supplying public libraries at discounts ranging from 25 to over 40 percent. Moreover, most bookstores have always been too small even to aspire to serve the very few public libraries with big reference and circulation departments. Only a few retailers have the resources to supply metropolitan libraries, and these retailers, who already carry a wide range of books, do not want the business.

NEW LIBRARY SOURCES   The importance of public library buying to trade publishing, then, has probably never been as great as some have thought, and despite somewhat greater expenditures by the libraries it may have actually declined in recent years. Some factors speeding this decline may also have reduced the importance of regular trade publishers to the libraries. Cass Canfield, board chairman of Harper's, speaking early in 1948 on trade publishers' "cultural responsibility," acknowledged that they must now exclude from their lists "volumes of a specialized nature and learned monographs."[5] Public libraries that buy such books must increasingly seek them elsewhere.

[5]*Publishers' Weekly*, April 3, 1948.

In recent years, not because their needs have been greater, but because trade publishers either have abandoned old fields or have failed to enter certain new ones, public libraries have been buying more books from university presses, from organizations such as the Foreign Policy Association, the Twentieth Century Fund, and the Brookings Institution, which publish their own work, from city and state governments, from the United Nations, and most important, from federal agencies. They have been also using greater numbers of timely pamphlets.

Material from these sources still is only an insignificant part of public library buying; yet as trade publishers' emphasis on best sellers grows and lists are made up increasingly with department store and subsidiary markets in mind, libraries will have to turn elsewhere for serious publications.

An illustration of how publishers have missed the business of an important and growing segment of the market was given by Robert West Howard, former editor of *Pathfinder* and the *Farm Journal*, who said that "professional publishers are asleep at the switch" in regard to the rural trade. According to *Publishers' Weekly*, March 28, 1948, he said:

Technological progress in farming has been accompanied by a desire for technological information [and regular publishers, in the main, have failed to meet this desire or other rural book needs]. Of 373 titles, recommended by the Department of Agriculture for rural reading, only 150 were put out by professional publishers. Of these, there were 36 by Macmillan, 20 by McGraw-Hill, 14 by Wiley, 12 by Harper, 6 by Knopf, 5 by Appleton Century, 4 each by Holt, Doubleday, Lippincott, Viking and Bruce, 3 by Scribner's, Barnes and Crofts. The rest were one's and two's; the remaining 222 titles were published by university presses and government presses.

Most of these 222 titles, though not large quantities of them, must have been acquired by all metropolitan libraries, and some by public libraries in rural and smaller urban areas. Howard should have pointed out, however, that a large proportion of the government's publications were and are available free of charge.

THE PUBLISHERS' TERMS   Though new sources are supplying increasing numbers of library books, the public libraries must continue to buy most of their books from regular trade publishers and virtually on their terms. Since most publishers will sell directly only to the largest libraries and most retailers can supply only the smallest, libraries as a rule buy from big wholesalers. Probably this is most economical. Wholesalers carry books of practically all publishers; they can easily fill large, small, and mixed orders; they are more centrally located than are most bookstores and have easier access to publishers' stocks; they save libraries ordering time, complicated bookkeeping, and much other clerical work.

For all this, of course, wholesalers charge; though they get most of their library business by offering better discounts than those of publishers and retailers, on some books and some small orders their discounts are as low as 10 percent. Some big public libraries, such as that of Chicago, buy almost exclusively from one big wholesaler—the winner in each year's competitive bidding for the library contract. Other libraries, among which the New York Public Library is outstanding, bargain with publishers, wholesalers, and retailers, and buy where they can do best. For such libraries and for smaller ones free to buy in the best markets, the American Booksellers Association's *Book Buyer's Handbook*, referred to previously, is a very useful guide.

Some trade publishers say that public libraries are consumers, that they give no service to publishers, that they compete unfairly with booksellers, and that for these reasons even those that buy in volume deserve no discounts whatever. The libraries, of course, dispute this.[6] They also object to the declining physical quality of books. Flimsy bindings, especially on juveniles, sharply reduce the number of times books can circulate. Margins have been so reduced that rebinding has become more difficult and more costly. Some books have no jackets, further shortening the life of cheap bindings.

Certain bookbinders and wholesalers, among them the Huntting Company and the Library Book House, deal largely with libraries. Before the war they were able to get from most publishers printed sheets of new books, which they themselves bound in durable, if unattractive, library cloths. This saved libraries much money on books they would otherwise have had to buy at full price, only to have the publishers' weak bindings removed at once and the book rebound for library use. It also saved the libraries the cost of rebinding many other books whose regular covers would quickly have worn out. During the war, often at the behest of the manufacturers, many publishers discontinued the practice of pulling sheets for library binding, and some have not resumed it. Thus, appreciable savings which were possible before the war are no longer possible for libraries.

To stretch their book-buying budgets, public libraries have been planning changes in buying practices. Virtually all the proposals are aimed at some method by which groups of libraries may pool orders for books all must buy and thus gain for each economies of purchasing in large quantities.

One widely discussed plan is regional co-operative buying, by which neighboring library systems hope to get bigger discounts from wholesalers and even to attract publishers

---

[6]Though now somewhat out of date, the best discussion of library discounts and their relation to bookselling generally is Orman, "Library Discount Control."

themselves.[7] Other plans entail some kind of "library book club." One suggestion, similar to the ABA's "leased plate project," is for a large number of libraries or the American Library Association to rent plates from publishers at the same low rates given commercial clubs, then to produce their own books and distribute them almost at cost to member libraries. A second idea is for groups of libraries or the ALA to guarantee to regular publishers a considerable minimum of sales of new books with uncertain market appeal and of backlist items (for replacement) which would otherwise be allowed to go out of print. By giving publishers some advantages of large editions, this plan would aim to induce them, with little risk to themselves, to produce certain books at low prices for special library needs.

A third variation of the club idea is more revolutionary. This proposes that groups of libraries or the ALA shall purchase reprint rights to books in great demand at libraries and issue them in pocket-size paper-bound editions. Some librarians now oppose the use of such books, but probably will not hold out long against them; libraries that have tried them have found that borrowers are much interested in them, especially the younger library users. Moreover, they are so inexpensive, even in the commercial market, that they can be bought and loaned for less than the cost to the libraries of the clerical work required in merely preparing regular hard-cover books for lending—an operation often almost as costly as the average hard-cover book itself.

Before most of these plans can be adopted, legal restrictions that now hamstring library buying and make many libraries undesirable customers will have to be removed. Resistance among librarians themselves will also have to be overcome;

[7]On the problems and implications of regionalism see Oliver Garceau, *Public Library Government*, New York, Columbia University Press, 1949, a study made for the Public Library Inquiry.

some librarians, for example, abhor the idea that anyone else should select a single book for their collections. Among publishers, too, a new spirit of co-operation with libraries will have to be won.

Perhaps the strongest incentive to libraries to improve their buying methods arises from the inadequacy of the budgets with which they are expected to serve their niggardly communities well. Yet most of these improvements, especially in so far as they require book industry co-operation, are likely to go untried as long as *total* library budgets remain at their present low level. Average annual budgets of less than seventy cents per capita—in eight states they were less than thirty cents in 1945—leave little for the purchase of new books.

It is true that library book budgets are increasing, but it is also true that the amount of public library buying will not soon be great enough to influence appreciably the output of serious books by commercial publishers. This is all the more reason for librarians to make the most of whatever influence they now have; but much more important, it is all the more reason why the *public* libraries should join with *other* libraries so as to mobilize *all* library purchasing power. Only in this way can they establish a market large enough and stable enough for a publishing policy to serve it. At the present time only one library agency seems capable of making the attempt —the American Library Association—and it does not yet speak for the whole profession.

The librarians, furthermore, will have to unite on a common policy of book selection. There must be some general consensus as to what they want in the way of important books. This would seem to be a large order, and it would certainly reverse the present trend, according to which libraries tend to follow the commercial market and its cultivation of best sellers. Difficult as it is to know what writing has lasting importance, wide usefulness, or social value, to the layman it would seem that such knowledge and judgment should be part of a professional librarian's basic equipment. If he can so use it as to create a market for good books, he will contribute not only to his own satisfaction but also to that of most publishers and of readers everywhere.

A NOTE ON METHOD AND SOURCES

LITTLE EFFORT is made in this book to supply elementary information concerning the management of the different segments of the book industry. For such information the reader is referred to *The Truth about Publishing,* by Sir Stanley Unwin, first published by George Allen & Unwin, Ltd., in London, in 1926, and issued in the United States the following year by Houghton Mifflin. Though this book was "completely revised" in 1946, it still contains much obsolete data and some that even when they were fresh were less representative of American than of conservative English practices. There has never been a good primer on American publishing; until one is written, Unwin's work must serve.

In the present book the emphasis is on the changing nature of American trade publishing, especially the publishing of adult books. I should have liked to write more about American education and American literacy, with special reference to book reading in a democracy. Much remains to be said, too, about censorship and intimidation and the climate in which these blights take root and flourish. The use of American books abroad in the postwar period is a topic about which nothing has been said here; probably it deserves a volume to itself. There are few available books of merit on any of these themes; original research on them was beyond the scope of the present work.

The greater part of the research for this book was done in the fall and winter, 1947–48, and an early draft, in the form of a report to the director of the Public Library Inquiry, was written the following spring. Since then relevant new information has been used as it has come to my attention. In a few instances such information has altered my interpretations and emphases and caused me to recast certain sections. Had the publication date more closely followed my first writing of the book (a difficult achievement for almost any book, which makes books in general rather unsatisfactory vehicles for discussions of current events), probably I should also have made other statements a little differently. Yet I believe the main trend of recent events in the book industry has only tended more strongly to justify most of my earlier views.

Most of the research for the present book took the form of interviews with people in the book industry. I feel safe in saying that in no other way, except possibly by the use of elaborate and extremely costly written questionnaires, could the material have been gathered for a general study of this industry—or of any other made up mainly of small companies issuing few public reports and not recently the subject of governmental or any other broad investigations.

Nevertheless, virtually all the quotations in this book are from printed sources.[1] A few of the quotations are from such reliable authorities that they may be taken as the best available evidence of the existence of certain situations or of the meaning of certain events. Most frequently, however, quotations have been used simply to illustrate conditions, points of view, interpretations; their evidence has sometimes been accepted and other times rejected, in each case on the basis of other kinds of data—oral or written opinions of individual experts, the consensus of acknowledged authorities, original documents, and the findings of special studies.

Publishers' Weekly, the industry's informative trade paper, has been the most frequent source of the quotations used in this book and of other data as well. Its 75th Anniversary issue, January 18, 1947, contains what is probably the best history of American trade publishing between the two wars. *Bookbinding and Book Production*, the book manufacturers' journal, has also been useful. The *Saturday Review of Literature* and the daily "Book Notes" and Sunday book sections of the New York *Times* and the New York *Herald Tribune* have contributed much.

For regular book industry information aside from that in book

[1] I wish to thank the publishers of these sources for permission to quote from them; full acknowledgement to author and publisher is made in the text or footnote in each case.

reviews, *Time*, among general periodicals, and *Tide*, among trade papers in other industries, have probably been most fruitful. *Harper's*, the *Atlantic*, the *New Yorker*, the *Nation*, and the *New Republic* occasionally have articles on book industry subjects. *Fortune* has had at least four full-scale stories on trade publishing: on Simon & Schuster, January, 1934; on Doubleday, February, 1936; on New York City publishers, July, 1939; and on the industry generally, November, 1943, the last by the author of the present work. Other magazine and newspaper sources occasionally used are given in text and footnotes and may be found through the index.

Among official industry publications, most useful have been the monthly *Bulletin* of the American Booksellers Association and the irregular releases of the American Book Publishers Council, especially its statistical reports. Among official United States Government publications, the various reports of the Bureau of the Census, particularly that for 1945, referred to in Chapter I and in Appendix B, have been informative. Useful, also, has been *Public Library Statistics, 1944–45*, Bulletin 1947, No. 12, of the Federal Security Agency, Office of Education (Government Printing Office, 1947). There is illuminating testimony by book industry spokesmen in *Hearings* before the Committee on Post Office and Civil Service, House of Representatives, Eightieth Congress, First Session, March and April, 1947 (Government Printing Office, 1947).

Some of the other publications of the Public Library Inquiry (listed elsewhere in this book), especially those by Bernard Berelson and James L. McCamy, bear closely upon book publishing problems; for publisher-library relations all are useful.

By far the best book on American trade publishing is the *Economic Survey of the Book Industry, 1930–1931*, written by O. H. Cheney and his staff for the National Association of Book Publishers, a predecessor of the present American Book Publishers Council. Few books on other American industries approach this one in authority and foresight; its flinty style once singed more publishers than it enlightened, but among the present generation of executives the demand has been great enough for it so that R. R. Bowker & Co. is planning to reissue it in 1949.

Besides Cheney and Unwin, the following books have proved useful. The list, of course, does not aim at completeness. It contains few memoirs of publishers, agents, or authors. Though some memoirs have cast light on publishers' or agents' relations with famous authors, almost without exception such books are anecdotal in style and tell little of the structure of the book industry and the conditions under which it has functioned at any time.

Berreman, Joel van M. "Factors Affecting the Sale of Modern Books of Fiction." Unpublished Ph.D. dissertation, Stanford University, 1940.

Book and Magazine Guild. Report on the Salary Survey of the Book Publishing Industry. New York, the Guild, 1940.

Canby, Henry Seidel. American Memoir. Boston, Houghton, 1947. By one of the founders of the *Saturday Review* and a judge of the Book-of-the-Month Club since its inception.

Duffus, R. L. Books; Their Place in a Democracy. Boston, Houghton, 1930.

—— Our Starving Libraries. Boston, Houghton, 1933.

Editions for the Armed Services, Inc.; a History; together with the Complete List of 1,324 Books Published for American Armed Forces Overseas. New York, issued by the Editions, 1948. The history chapter in this volume "is a slightly condensed version of a chapter which will appear in a forthcoming history of the Army Library Service in World War II written by John Jamieson under the joint sponsorship of the Carnegie Corporation of New York and the American Library Association."

Farrell, James T. Literature and Morality. New York, Vanguard, 1947. Contains his "The Fate of Writing in America," also separately published as a pamphlet by New Directions.

Hackett, Alice Payne. Fifty Years of Best Sellers, 1895–1945. New York, Bowker, 1945.

History of the Council on Books in Wartime 1942–1946. New York, the Council, 1946.

Lehmann-Haupt, Hellmut, and others. The Book in America; a History of the Making, the Selling, and the Collecting of Books in the United States. New York, Bowker, 1939. This is the only lengthy history of this subject; for the period since 1890 it is sketchy; nowhere in it is publishing treated as an integral part of the whole culture.

Link, Henry C., and Harry A. Hopf. People and Books; a Study of Reading and Book-Buying Habits. New York, The Book Industry Committee of the Book Manufacturers Institute, 1946. A disappointing and often misleading book.

McMurtrie, Douglas C. The Book; the Story of Printing and Bookmaking. New York, Covici-Friede, 1937.

Mott, Frank Luther. Golden Multitudes; the Story of Best Sellers in the United States. New York, Macmillan, 1947.

Myrick, Frank B. A Primer in Book Production. New York, Bookbinding and Book Production, 1945.

Nicholson, Margaret. A Manual of Copyright Practice for Writers, Publishers, and Agents. New York, Oxford University Press, 1945.

Orman, Oscar C. "Library Discount Control." Chicago, American Library Association, 1941. Mimeographed.

Waples, Douglas. People and Print; Social Aspects of Reading in the Depression. Chicago, University of Chicago Press, 1938.

Wilson, Louis R. The Geography of Reading; a Study of the Distribution and Status of Libraries in the United States. Chicago, University of Chicago Press, 1938. An excellent book with considerable information about book markets in the thirties.

Wilson, Louis R., ed. The Practice of Book Selection; Papers presented before the Library Institute at the University of Chicago, July 31 to August 13, 1939. Chicago, University of Chicago Press, 1940. Particularly relevant to the book industry are the papers by Adolph Kroch and Frederic G. Melcher, though most of the other papers contain useful information.

These books have all been helpful, but the present volume could not have been written at all, as I have said, were it not for the large number of people in the book industry and in others related to it who were so generous with time and liberal with information when interviewed. Many of them took additional hours to read this book in manuscript; a few even reread it in galley proof.

I know that some of these people disagree with much that I say, and most disagree with some of it. For errors of fact or interpretation the fault is mine. For what I have chosen to write the responsibility lies with me alone.

The following members of regular trade houses have all been helpful (position and company in most instances are as of the period of interviewing): Doubleday and Co.: Thomas R. Burns, general manager and sales manager; Ken McCormick, editor-in-chief; A. Milton Runyon, vice-president; Jay Tower, publicity. E. P. Dutton and Co.: Sherman Baker, editor. Farrar, Straus & Co.: Roger W. Straus, Jr., president. Harper & Bros.: Raymond C. Harwood, secretary, treasurer, and general manager; William H. Rose, Jr., director of advertising, promotion, and sales. Henry Holt and Co.: Joseph A. Brandt, president; Joseph Duffy, sales manager (later in charge of research for the Ohio Plan). Houghton Mifflin Co.: Mrs. Jean Poindexter Colby, juvenile editor; Mrs. Dorothy DeSantillana, managing editor. Alfred A. Knopf, Inc.: Sidney R. Jacobs, production manager; Carleton G. Power, sales manager (earlier with World Publishing Co.). Little, Brown & Co.: Angus Cameron, vice-president and editor. The Macmillan Co.: George P. Brett, Jr., president; Donald P. Geddes and James Putnam, editors; J. Randall Williams, sales manager. McGraw-Hill Book Co.: Hugh J. Kelly, vice-president. W. W. Norton & Co.: Storer B. Lunt, president. Pellegrini & Cudahy, Inc.: Sheila Cudahy, vice-president and editor. G. P. Putnam's Sons: Melville Minton, president (first president of the American Book Publishers Council). Random House: Frank Taylor, editor (later with MGM). Rinehart & Co.: Stahley Thompson, production manager (earlier, manager of the Armed Services Editions). Simon & Schuster: Albert R. Leventhal, vice-president and sales manager. William Sloane Associates: Keith W. Jennison, sales manager; Helen K. Taylor, managing editor. Viking Press: Marshall A. Best, general manager; Milton B. Glick, production manager; May Massee, juvenile editor.

Among reprinters.—Grosset & Dunlap: John O'Connor, president (also board chairman of Bantam Books); Manuel Siwek, sales manager. The New American Library of World Literature, Inc.: Philip Album and Richard J. Crohn, sales managers; Kurt Enoch, president; Victor Weybright, chairman and editor. Pocket Books: Freeman Lewis, vice-president.

Among book clubs.—The Book Find Club: George Braziller, director; Edwin Seaver, publicity and promotion (earlier with the Book-of-the-Month Club). The Book-of-the-Month Club: Harry Dale, production manager; Amy Loveman, head of the Editorial Department (also secretary of the *Saturday Review of Literature*); Harry Scherman, president; Meredith Wood, vice-president and treasurer. The Literary Guild (and other Doubleday clubs): John Beecroft, editor. The People's Book Club: Sanford Cobb, in charge of books at Sears, Roebuck & Co.

At university presses.—University of Chicago Press: William T. Couch, director. Princeton University Press: Datus C. Smith, Jr., director and editor.

Among literary agents.—Harold Matson: Donald Congdon. Gossett Studios: Margaret Gossett and Mary Elting. A. and S. Lyons, Inc.: Mavis McIntosh. Constance Smith (independent). Harold Ober: Ivan von Auw, Jr.

Among distributors.—The American News Co.: Harold E. Williams, vice-president in charge of the book department. The Baker & Taylor Co.: Michael A. Corrigan, vice-president in charge of sales. A. C. McClurg & Co.: Guy Kendall, head of the book department. Brentano's, Inc.: Joseph A. Margolies, vice-president. Kroch's Bookstores: Carl Kroch.

At advertising agencies.—Green-Brodie: Alan Green, partner (also advertising manager at Viking Press). Sussman & Sugar, Inc.: Aaron Sussman, president.

At industry publications.—*Publishers' Weekly:* Louis C. Greene, vice-president and advertising manager; Frederic G. Melcher, president and editor. Virginia Kirkus Bookshop Service: Virginia Kirkus, director. H. W. Wilson, Co.: H. W. Wilson, president.

At industry associations.—American Book Publishers Council: Donald S. Cameron, acting managing director; Harry F. West, managing director (later resigned). American Booksellers Association: Gilbert E. Goodkind, executive secretary. Association of American University Presses: Chester Kerr, director of the "Survey of University Presses." The Authors' League of America: Luise M. Sillcox, executive secretary.

At the American Library Association.—Carl Milam, executive secretary (later resigned).

Among librarians.—The New York Public Library: Mrs. Edith A. Busby, superintendent of book ordering.

For the opportunity to write this book I thank my friends Bernard Berelson and Robert D. Leigh. For assistance in carrying it to completion I am grateful to Mrs. Lois A. Murkland, administrative assistant of the Public Library Inquiry, and her staff. For criticism of the manuscript at different stages, and for other assistance I am indebted to many friends not in the book industry: Roger Butterfield, Thomas C. Cochran, C. DeWitt Hardy, Beatrice Kevitt, Richard Hofstadter, Mulford Martin, C. Wright Mills, Henry M. Silver, and to the members of the Social Science Research Council's Committee for the Public Library Inquiry. My wife, Virginia Buckner Miller, has read and criticized the manuscript of this book I suppose as often as I have myself. For her sustained interest in it I express my appreciation.

W.M.

APPENDIX B

SOME BOOK INDUSTRY STATISTICS

TABLE 1

AMERICAN BOOK PRODUCTION 1929–48, BY TOTAL NUMBER OF
TITLES OF NEW EDITIONS AND NEW BOOKS[a]

Year	Total Titles	Year	Total Titles
1929	10,187	1939	10,640
1930	10,027	1940	11,328
1931	10,307	1941	11,112
1932	9,035	1942	9,525
1933	8,092	1943	8,325
1934	8,198	1944	6,970
1935	8,766	1945	6,548
1936	10,436	1946	7,735
1937	10,912	1947	9,182
1938	11,067	1948	9,897

[a]*Publishers' Weekly*, annual summary number, usually third issue in January
of succeeding year.

Table 2

American Book Production 1939–48, by Subject and Number of Titles[a]

International Classification	Total 1939	CHANGE[b] FROM THE PRECEDING YEAR								
		1940	1941	1942	1943	1944	1945	1946	1947	1948
Philosophy, ethics	102	8	12	−38	131	−59	51	−15	98	18
Religion, theology	697	146	−179	−8	−55	−60	−103	92	100	47
Sociology, economics	854	22	−15	−241	−35	−264	−20	10	76	74
Law	163	39	−12	−78	−34	10	29	7	90	17
Education	315	34	−4	−128	39	−112	−20	23	47	5
Philology	286	33	19	−58	−66	−35	−28	−43	48	−7
Science	523	−30	−2	−94	52	−117	9	9	92	150
Technical, military	452	159	130	50	−106	−144	−165	−39	56	73
Medicine, hygiene	431	41	20	−49	−112	−58	29	−2	22	111
Agriculture, gardening	129	10	−29	−10	−2	−54	6	5	42	65
Domestic economy	100	−6	32	−14	5	−6	5	28	57	−18
Business	357	45	−12	−129	−115	−26	32	64	12	−5
Fine arts	288	−66	32	−67	−12	−35	38	89	−18	87
Music	124	0	−17	−40	9	−36	15	16	23	10
Games, sports	219	−37	−38	5	−60	−9	−12	66	34	31
General literature	584	−48	−31	−105	−99	−34	−2	72	63	73
Poetry, drama	653	85	85	−229	−201	14	−27	61	70	52
Fiction	1,547	189	−25	−48	−185	−138	−47	429	244	−323
Juvenile	949	35	19	−139	−174	−45	46	186	56	−4
History	804	49	−100	−107	−107	−9	−187	16	54	90
Geography, travel	357	−49	−36	−13	−44	−64	−53	35	63	18
Biography	628	19	−48	−57	−69	−51	−30	64	62	−5
Miscellaneous	78	10	−17	10	40	−23	12	14	56	156
Total all books	10,640	11,328	11,112	9,525	8,325	6,970	6,548	7,735	9,182	9,897
Total new editions	1,625	1,813	1,775	1,739	1,561	1,163	1,162	1,565	1,939	2,090
Total new books	9,015	9,515	9,337	7,786	6,764	5,807	5,386	6,710	7,243	7,807

[a] *Publishers' Weekly*, annual summary number, usually third issue in January of succeeding year.

TABLE 3

AMERICAN BOOK PRODUCTION 1929–45, BY SUBJECT AND NUMBER OF COPIES[a]

Census Classification	1929	1933	1939	1945
Juvenile	36,885,167	22,346,400	34,848,416	
Fiction	26,880,062	11,527,519	14,811,181	
Religion, philosophy	12,796,741	6,764,254	6,613,606	
Bibles, testaments, etc.	4,829,208	666,448	8,053,814	
Poetry, drama	4,048,227	1,989,647	1,499,477	
Law	2,942,176	1,812,946	2,356,395	
Biography	2,714,090	1,449,315	2,384,647	
Science, technology	2,294,660	1,611,642	3,432,642	
History	1,950,495	831,858	2,306,829	
Medicine	1,932,909	674,763	1,868,892	
Travel, geography	1,725,561	885,535	1,482,138	
Fine arts	1,133,855	335,362	590,885	
Sociology, economics	1,052,049	1,113,513	886,751	
Agriculture, etc.	688,810	131,382	1,018,809	
Miscellaneous	32,270,478[b]	7,805,245	16,767,072	
Not reported by class	...	599,779	...	
Texts (for school use)	80,189,935	48,070,083	63,274,758	
Reference	...[c]	...[c]	6,716,403	
Bluebooks, catalogues, directories, etc.	...[b]	2,174,222	7,724,351	
Total	214,334,423	110,789,913	176,637,066	428,832,884

[a]For 1929–39 figures are from U.S. Bureau of the Census, *Census of Manufactures*, 1939, and represent book "production"; for 1945 the total is from *The Book Publishing Industry in the U.S., 1945*, published as part of the "Facts for Industry" series, by the Bureau of the Census, and represents sales by publishers, not production. On the definition of a "book" in these tables see pp. 21–22 above. See Table 4 for breakdown of 1945 total.

[b]For 1929 "Miscellaneous" includes "Bluebooks, catalogues," etc.

[c]No data for these years.

TABLE 4

AMERICAN BOOK SALES, 1945, BY COPIES AND PUBLISHERS' DOLLAR RECEIPTS[a]

ORIGINAL EDITIONS

NUMBER OF COPIES SOLD

Census Classification	Hard-bound	Paper-bound	Total	Total Receipts
Trade	70,928,103	34,272,700	105,200,803	$74,359,927
Text	53,599,722	14,503,404	68,103,126	59,907,341
Religious	18,383,138	21,613,610	39,996,748	18,658,042
Subscription & mail order	13,279,374	1,630,440	14,909,814	47,629,773
Technical & professional	7,412,030	5,835,150	13,247,180	20,386,062
Other	1,243,941	7,968,223	9,212,164	4,544,133
Total	164,846,308	85,823,527	250,669,835	$225,485,278

REPRINT EDITIONS

Trade	49,464,670	82,951,552	132,416,222	$24,794,837
Text	358,855	230,879	589,734	532,237
Religious	1,339,414	1,663,104	3,002,518	2,217,178
Subscription & mail order	31,543,333	3,125,035	34,668,368	38,329,548
Technical & professional	112,065	. . .	112,065	617,347
Other	99,566	7,274,576	7,374,142	1,383,955
Total	82,917,903	95,245,146	178,163,049	$67,875,102
Total of original and reprint editions	247,764,211	181,068,673	428,832,884	$293,360,380

[a]Based on reports of 1,080 book publishers, as reported in *The Book Publishing Industry in the U.S., 1945.* See Table 3 note *a*, and also pp. 22–23.

TABLE 5

THE AVERAGE PERCENTAGE INCREASE IN MANUFACTURING COST
ITEMS, AND THE HIGHEST AND LOWEST REPORTED BY 27
PUBLISHERS, FROM JANUARY, 1942, TO APRIL, 1947[a]

Item	Number of Copies	PERCENTAGE OF INCREASE		
		AVERAGE	HIGHEST REPORTED	LOWEST REPORTED
Paper				
Antique		45	87	34
Offset		37	56	24
Coated		45	87	5
Linotype composition		77	138	33
Electrotypes (plates)		65	100	15
Printing				
Offset	1,000	66	104	35
	2,500	58	94	29
	5,000	53	94	22
	10,000	45	81	19
	25,000	39	75	13
Letter press	1,000	58	107	21
	2,500	57	106	21
	5,000	55	93	22
	10,000	54	85	21
	25,000	54	98	20
Cloth binding	1,000	61	120	18
	2,500	62	100	11
	5,000	60	100	9
	10,000	59	100	8
	25,000	58	97	8

[a]American Book Publishers Council, *Statistical Report,* 1946–47.

TABLE 6

DISTRIBUTION BY REGIONS AND STATES OF AMERICAN BOOKSTORES,
MAJOR BOOK-CLUB MEMBERSHIPS, AND ORIGINAL EDITIONS OF
TRADE BOOKS[a]

Region and State	Percentage of Bookstores[b]	Percentage of Publishers' Direct Sales[c]	Percentage of Major Book-Club Members[d]	Percentage of U.S. Population[e]
Northeastern				
New York	17.4	27.0	12.6	9.8
Pennsylvania	6.7	5.6	7.6	7.0
Massachusetts	4.7	5.6	3.9	3.4
New Jersey	1.7	1.8	6.0	3.1
Connecticut	2.0	1.4	1.9	1.4
Rhode Island	0.6	0.3	0.4	0.5
Maine	0.4	0.3	0.7	0.6
Vermont	0.4	0.2	0.3	0.3
New Hampshire	0.4	0.2	0.4	0.4
Total	34.3	42.4	33.8	26.5
East Central				
Illinois	5.5	9.3	7.2	5.7
Ohio	5.2	4.5	4.8	5.3
Michigan	3.9	2.9	5.3	4.6
Wisconsin	1.6	1.3	1.9	2.2
Indiana	1.8	1.2	2.3	2.6
Total	18.0	19.2	21.5	20.4
Southeastern				
District of Columbia	1.5	2.0	1.3	0.6
Tennessee	1.5	1.8	1.1	2.1
Maryland	1.6	1.3	1.6	1.6
Virginia	1.5	1.2	2.1	2.1
Florida	2.4	1.0	1.6	1.7
Georgia	1.0	0.9	1.1	2.2
North Carolina	1.6	0.8	1.6	2.6
Kentucky	0.7	0.5	0.9	2.0
Alabama	1.0	0.5	1.0	2.0
West Virginia	0.7	0.4	1.1	1.3
South Carolina	0.5	0.3	0.9	1.4
Mississippi	0.5	0.2	0.5	1.5
Delaware	0.1	0.2	0.5	0.2
Total	14.6	11.1	15.3	21.3

TABLE 6 (continued)

Region and State	Percentage of Bookstores[b]	Percentage of Publishers' Direct Sales[c]	Percentage of Major Book-Club Members[d]	Percentage of U.S. Population[e]
West Central				
Missouri	2.4	2.8	1.9	2.7
Texas	3.6	2.6	3.9	5.0
Minnesota	1.5	1.8	1.4	2.0
Iowa	1.5	0.9	1.4	1.8
Louisiana	1.0	0.9	0.9	1.8
Oklahoma	1.1	0.7	1.0	1.6
Kansas	1.1	0.6	1.2	1.3
Nebraska	0.7	0.4	0.5	0.9
Arkansas	0.6	0.3	0.6	1.4
North Dakota	0.2	0.1	0.3	0.4
South Dakota	0.2	0.1	0.3	0.4
Total	13.9	11.2	13.4	19.3
Western				
California	12.0	9.2	10.0	6.8
Washington	2.3	3.4	1.7	1.6
Oregon	1.0	1.4	1.2	1.0
Colorado	1.0	0.6	0.7	0.8
Utah	0.4	0.4	0.4	0.5
New Mexico	0.3	0.3	0.3	0.4
Arizona	0.6	0.2	0.5	0.5
Montana	0.7	0.2	0.4	0.3
Idaho	0.5	0.2	0.4	0.3
Wyoming	0.3	0.1	0.2	0.2
Nevada	0.1	0.1	0.2	0.1
Total	19.2	16.1	16.0	12.5

[a]There are no good figures for these subjects; those given here seem to be the best available, and in most instances the latest.

[b]This column based on the 3,041 stores described above in the text, p. 89.

[c]Based on sales to retailers, individuals, and libraries (but not to wholesalers) in 1946 by 20 publishers with total sales of $30 million, as reported in the American Book Publishers Council 1946–47 *Statistical Report*. The Council's 1947–48 report had similar figures for 1947 sales, but based on many fewer publishers with much smaller sales. It was decided to use those of the earlier report. Also see text, pp. 97–98.

[d]The figures are for 1947. See text pp. 117–18.

[e]Based on census estimates of 1946 population.

INDEX

THE FOLLOWING VOLUMES IN THE PUBLIC LIBRARY INQUIRY SERIES ARE PUBLISHED
BY THE COLUMBIA UNIVERSITY PRESS.

Leigh, Robert D., The Public Library in the United States.

Berelson, Bernard, The Library's Public.

Bryan, Alice I., The Public Librarian.

Garceau, Oliver, The Public Library in the Political Process.

McCamy, James L., Government Publications for the Citizen.

Miller, William, The Book Industry.

Waldron, Gloria, The Information Film.

THE FOLLOWING MIMEOGRAPHED REPORTS TO THE DIRECTOR OF THE INQUIRY MAY
BE PURCHASED FROM THE AGENCIES INDICATED.

Armstrong, Charles M., "Money for Libraries; a report on library finance."
New York (230 Park Avenue), Social Science Research Council.

Klapper, Joseph T., "Effects of Mass Media." New York (15 Amsterdam
Avenue), Bureau of Applied Social Research, Columbia University.

Luening, Otto, "Music Materials and the Public Library; an analysis of the
role of the public library in the field of music." New York (230 Park
Avenue), Social Science Research Council.

Pierce, Watson O'D., "Work Measurement in Public Libraries." New York
(230 Park Avenue), Social Science Research Council.

"Public Library and the People, The; a national survey done for the
Public Library Inquiry." Ann Arbor, Michigan, Survey Research Center,
the University of Michigan.